CRYSTAL PALACE VISTAS

Crystal Palace

ROGER HUTCHINGS

CRYSTAL PALACE VISTAS

Vista: a view or prospect ...
figuratively, a mental view or vision
of a far reaching nature
– *Oxford Dictionary*

Roger Hutchings

The Book Guild Ltd
Sussex, England

The Book Guild Ltd,
25 High Street,
Lewes, Sussex

First published 1999
© Roger Hutchings 1999

Set in New Baskerville
Typesetting by IML Typographers, Chester
Printed in Great Britain by
Bookcraft (Bath) Ltd, Avon

A catalogue record for this book is
available from the British Library

ISBN 1 85776 470 6

TO MARY
for her patience
and to
Zara and Cathérine
because they sought
and found me

'I can ruin a night's sleep by suddenly, in the dark, thinking about some particular time in my life. It is as if I had driven a mine shaft down through layers of the past and must explore, re-live, remember, reconsider, until daylight delivers me.'

William Maxwell

'... the lit-up theatre of childhood puts the later years into a half-light, so that we seem to have lived the rest of our lives as a mere audience of our own past.'

V.S. Pritchett

'Nostalgia isn't what it used to be.'

Groucho Marx

Nostalgia is a widely variable human experience. To some it is unknown, to others it occurs briefly and hazily, but to the confirmed daydreamer it is an obsession that becomes increasingly vivid with age. These present reminiscences are nominally an account of childhood in a South London suburb during the nineteen twenties. Its characters, including the narrator, are unimportant: if the text is of interest to later generations, it will be for its glimpses of the social history of a brief era that in many respects was more representative of the nineteenth century than of the twentieth.

I knew when it was Armistice Day in 1918 because I heard my parents talking about it over breakfast. As soon as my father left for the office my mother sent me up to the end of the garden to fetch a bean pole. This was to be an improvised flagstaff to bear a Union Jack that she told me had been kept in readiness since the outbreak of war. We took it up to the front bedroom and wedged the pole under the window sash for the flag to hang outside. All along the road there were flags fluttering from other windows, or being set in place.

I was proud to be sent for the beanpole because for some time previously I had been forbidden to go into the garden on my own as the back fence had blown down, and I suppose that my mother feared I would be tempted to stray beyond our boundary. The abutting garden was of a house in the next road whose residents she held in high esteem, so that the slightest breach of manners was to be avoided. That road faced away from London and towards the nearby county boundary of Kent and the open countryside, whereas the parallel roads in the other direction were closer to London and so less desirable in her estimation. This was like an inversion of an historic English north-south prejudice: nations to the south – France and Spain in particular – were despised, so logically the Scots to the north must be admirable. To reinforce my mother's stand, a few doors beyond the house with the broken garden fence there was known to reside a member of the House of Lords. My father was unimpressed by this and commented that his Lordship 'must be a waster and a dropout to be living in a neighbourhood like ours.'

A week or so after the Armistice my parents and some of our neighbours organised a street party, repeated annually for several years. For me this was doubly memorable because my mother strongly disapproved of children playing outside in the road. The only other annual celebration that compared with it was on Guy Fawkes night, with a grand communal bonfire around which to let off our fireworks, except for two couples, said to be Roman Catholics, who stayed indoors and kept their blinds drawn. This public get-together continued each year until the road surface was macadamised over the old cobblestones and the fire melted the tarmac, bringing a reproving warning from the Council, so after that bonfires and fireworks were confined to back gardens.

*

My earliest recollection pre-dated Armistice Day by twelve months or so. My Grandmother Silverwood and Aunt Rene (my mother's younger sister) had arrived for the day just as the air-raid siren sounded, leaving a loaded shopping bag on the kitchen table as they rushed out to the back garden in response to a call from next door. Finding myself unexpectedly alone I stood on tiptoe to survey the table top. Pulling the shopping bag towards me, I explored its contents and drew out a string of sausages which I looped around my neck before joining the adults outside, where they were gazing up at a Zeppelin under attack by our planes. It passed out of sight over the rooftops and was subsequently brought down in flames beyond London in Essex. My aunt was then said to suffer a bout of hysteria, but whether from relief at the 'all clear' siren or at the sight of my neckwear I never knew. In retrospect, it seems odd now that during the First World War the word siren was pronounced 'sireen', and that wartime rations were called 'rayshuns'.

*   *   *

Although the Crystal Palace dominated the skylines of the South London suburbs, and indeed of a vast area of south-east England, it was sadly obscured by the rooftops where I lived as a child. I first saw the Palace, distantly, from the Shirley Hills of South Croydon, where I was sometimes taken for picnic outings on fine weekends. The Hills seemed to rise as high as the Palace, and its towers were often enveloped in clouds that accentuated its magical presence. Even in winter darkness its unseen location was proclaimed by spectacular firework displays that illuminated the skies for miles around.

Throughout my childhood and adolescence every visit to the Crystal Palace was to enter into a world apart from everyday life, a realm of blissful contentment and delights. Music enveloped the vast building due to superb natural acoustics unaided by latter-day amplification. During each visit there would be a performance of either an orchestra, or the great theatre organ, or brass bands, of which regional and national contests were regularly held there. On a memorable occasion in my teens an impromptu performance took place one Saturday morning by Louis Armstrong and his full orchestra, then appearing at the nearby Penge Empire. 'Sounds don't travel any place better,' he was quoted as declaring.

Once inside the Palace there would always be something unexpected to be added to whatever was the purpose of the visit. On one occasion, for instance, I recall passing through an exhibition of fire engines while on our way to the circus. Another time, attending a pigeon show, there was a convention of harpists gathered in the amphitheatre with instruments of many shapes and sizes, from orchestral models to Welsh, Irish and Breton examples, and miniature hand-held harps from Paraguay. A visit to the Palace aquarium was an occasion I always enjoyed. It had been established, the first in the country, by Frank Buckland, the celebrated Victorian naturalist, whose brother Sir Henry was for many years the Crystal Palace's General Manager and was still in charge when I was a child.

One winter there was a South London Exhibition, similar to

the Ideal Home Exhibition at Olympia. It was announced to be the first of an annual series, but I do not recall a successor. The event was memorable for the music of a Hungarian gypsy orchestra and the solo performance of a cimbalom player. This instrument, resembling a zither but with bulbous-tipped sticks to strike its strings deserves greater recognition for its versatility. Between the wars an immigrant East Ender used to play one during lunchtime in the streets and squares of the City of London, and attracted crowds of appreciative listeners.

When the Crystal Palace was rebuilt in 1854 after the Great Exhibition in Hyde Park, it was said to be situated in Sydenham, although the Boroughs of Croydon, Lambeth and Southwark and the Urban District of Penge all converged at its site. Latterly, confusion was eliminated as the entire surrounding area became known as Crystal Palace, as it still is. The neighbouring shopping centre is distinguished for its concentration of public houses, of which there are still 17 within a radius of a couple of hundred yards.

The Palace originally had two railway stations bearing its name. The Low Level station provided direct access into the building by stairs or lift. A house outside, probably formerly for the station master, had become a chapel and the seat of a heterodox bishop who claimed succession from the schismatic Old Catholics of Holland. The High Level station (since demolished) connected with the interior by way of a long underground corridor, and this was the way we regularly used. The length of the corridor accentuated the anticipation, although there were sometimes distractions on the way by stalls set in its alcoves. I remember one, announced by a banner reading EDUCATIONAL TOYS, selling gyroscopes, humming tops, kaleidoscopes and boomerangs. Another sold Esperanto books and pamphlets, and another supplied a range of honeys imported by the Empire Marketing Board.

Our visits to the Palace during my early childhood were by tram, but later on we usually went by train. The last stretch of the tram route before we alighted was the steep rise up Anerley

4

Hill. This was no doubt the origin of my impression that Puff the Magic Dragon in the song of that title 'lived in a land called Anerley,' but I was eventually to discover that in fact it was Hanalei, on the Hawaiian island of Kanai.

Anerley was, and still is, a district with no defined boundaries or local authority or postal identity of that name, only a railway station. Indeed, it could realistically be described as an attitude of mind rather than a place: it is where many residents of Penge prefer to claim as their address.

*

The first visit to the Crystal Palace that I can remember was to a gala event of the Primrose League, a children's section of the Conservative Party. At this, and subsequent annual galas to which my mother took me for several years, the principal activity (apart from consuming lemonade and sticky buns) was a display by elder children bearing red, white and blue flags, who formed up on the main terrace to represent the Union Jack. I have since wondered why 'Primrose', and why the branch in which I was enrolled bore the name of 'Grantham Dames Habitation'. Who were these Dames, and why should a branch of the League be called a Habitation?

My next visit to the Palace was on the occasion of my Uncle Joe's demobilisation from the Royal Air Force in 1919. The building had been closed to the public during the war and was now the temporary repository of material destined to establish the Imperial War Museum. In consequence, the demobilisation procedures took place in crowded corridors crammed with shuffling queues. When we eventually came across my uncle, he had just been transformed into a civilian, uncomfortably clad in an ill-fitting suit of brown cloth. 'There was no other choice left,' he protested to us. I should explain that at this period men's serge or worsted suits were arbitrarily black, dark blue, or

5

grey: brown was unspeakable, at least for town wear, and was associated only with country-dwelling yokels. This one was speedily consigned to one of the local 'wardrobe' shops. These dealt in discarded clothing and personal effects, and were similar to latter-day charity shops. Outside the nearest one to home there was always a bin of old dentures, and I was revolted at the idea of prospective buyers rummaging through them to find an acceptable fit. I was relieved of this horror when it was explained to me that they were not for re-use but for the recovery of metals used in making them. A similar misconception arose when tin foil was being collected 'to make artificial limbs for ex-servicemen'. I could see that these were then made of wood, but I eventually understood that the foil collected would be sold to smelters to provide funds for the charities concerned.

*   *   *

We lived in Woodside, an area of South Norwood in the Borough of Croydon, although our postal address was London SE25. My Uncle Joe Silverwood and Aunt May lived next door, and a gap in the garden fence allowed me access to their house almost as if it were an extension of our own. This gave me much pleasure, as I was devoted to them, and they played a significant role in my upbringing.

Aunt May was regarded by the rest of the family into which she had married as an authority on matters of propriety and etiquette, as her mother had been in domestic service in a superior household. She brought some euphemistic expressions into the family that were adopted by my parents, notably 'attending the Wesleyan Chapel' for visits to the outdoor WC in a garden hut.

Uncle Joe's elder brother, Percy, was posted 'missing, believed killed' in France in 1917, and was never traced. I saw him only once, when he was home on leave. My mother and I were both convinced that he had survived, suffering loss of memory, but it was many years before we discovered that we shared this conviction. Finally, after some 50 years, I dreamt that he had died, and soon after my mother phoned me, saying 'I feel sure that poor Percy has passed on at last.'

For a brief period of my childhood there was a hawker of matches who plied at the kerbside in the High Street. He wore an Army officer's cap and tunic from which badges and medal ribbons had been conspicuously removed, and his face was concealed by a mask, protecting his identity and, supposedly, his shame. My mother referred to him as 'that poor devil'. I fantasised that he might be my lost Uncle Percy.

*

Next door to my uncle and aunt lived Mrs Newson, a war widow, whose only child Maud was about my age, but I had only slight contact with her. She was but tenuously in touch with reality, being in almost constant communication, often out loud, with unseen friends known to her as 'Winnie Boy' and 'Winnie Girl' and their baby brother, 'Juicy Boy'. Her mother had a reputation for odd behaviour, and I have been told that she was eventually certified insane after a siege of the home, during which gas and water supplies were cut off. She was said to have been found attempting suicide with her head in the oven, but had evidently forgotten that it was without gas. I never heard what happened to Maud.

The next neighbours in that direction were the Millwards, of whom my mother disapproved because they kept hens and pigeons in the back garden. Their son, Wally, was a few years older than me, and she was infuriated when he invited me to go with him on an errand to fetch chicken feed. She was doubly incensed because I had been warned against speaking to him and because the corn shop was in Albert Road, at the 'wrong end' of ours, and therefore, in her estimation, sure to be rough and dangerous for children.

Mr Millward was an engineer, an occupation my father held in low esteem on account of its five-year apprenticeship, which he contrasted unfavourably with the seven-years term served by a printer's compositor, the trade of one of his cousins, adding that it ensured a lifetime's employment. Later on, as an adult, I came to appreciate the reality of this, as in those days a 'time served' comp was virtually unsackable – although his livelihood could be lost at a nod if he infringed his union's regulations.

On the other side of the terrace to my uncle and aunt our next door neighbours were the Norris family, with two daughters older than me. I was supposed to enjoy playing with them, but their games and pastimes rarely appealed to me. For quite a time they were preoccupied with 'magic' painting. This involved outline pictures, black on white; each area, when wetted with a paintbrush dipped in plain water, became coloured as the paper dried. The girls wetted each part separately and left it to dry before proceeding with another, according to the instructions, but I wetted the entire picture to get an instant result, which they denounced as cheating. Their next craze was for autograph books. These were pocket-size volumes of multi-shade blank pages on which friends and acquaintances were invited to inscribe signed messages. In both girls' books most of the entries were identical, including the final one: 'By hook or by crook I'll be the last in this book.'

Between my parents and the Norrises there was a close friend-ship, and they passed many weekend evenings together, with sing-songs round the piano, individual 'turns', and party games. A surprising number of the residents in our road had pianos in their front rooms, however sparsely they were otherwise fur-nished. The possession of a piano had become a status symbol comparable to the role to be occupied by the upholstered three-piece suite in later years. Young girls, and some boys, were taught to play by the choirmaster of the parish church. These lessons, and home entertainment, fed the demand for sheet music, of which the two local music shops held copious stocks. In each of them prospective purchases could be tried out or demonstrated by an assistant, and one shop employed a skilled pianist to play popular pieces throughout Saturday afternoons and evenings. In warm weather the piano would be wheeled outside under the shop's awning to entertain passers-by and perhaps entice them inside to buy. Sheet music was also some-times hawked in the Saturday street market by a pianist and his vocalist partner, who wheeled their instrument there on a low trolley. Gramophone records were not stocked by the music shops, but a specialist dealer in central Croydon was devoted entirely to them. My Grandfather Silverwood and Uncle Joe were keen record collectors and would often spend several hours there on a Saturday, sampling them in the soundproofed listening booths, while the ladies shopped around the depart-ment stores.

Mr Norris was a skilled electrician and constructed some of the early radios – 'wireless sets' as they were then called. He made a primitive one for me, activated by a crystal and 'cat's whisker', on which I listened-in to the Children's Corner and heard my name read out on my birthday, followed by teatime dance music played by Carol Gibbons and his orchestra, relayed from the Savoy Hotel. This was in 1923, when programmes from the London station 2LO were produced by the British Broadcasting Company, which preceded the BBC. I wondered about the identity of 1LO until someone said that it was the Admiralty station broadcasting to warships at sea. Crystal sets required headphones; sets with loudspeakers needed valves and acid accumulators, which had to be taken on a hazardous journey to a garage when they needed to be recharged.

My mother and Mrs Norris usually took sit-down afternoon tea together, alternately in each other's kitchen or in fine summer weather outdoors. They took it in turn to make sandwiches, usually of tinned salmon or sardines, or ham. When it was ham I had corned beef, which my mother always explained to Mrs Norris was not that she was being mean, but because it was my preference.

On the other side of the Norris house lived a sad lady known to her neighbours as Ma Bacon, although she was apparently childless. According to my mother and Mrs Norris she was disgracefully inquisitive and a peeping eavesdropper, but I guess that she was lonely and bored and longed to be sharing in the neighbourliness she saw and heard next door, but leaving her isolated. Her husband was mostly away from home, reappearing after long intervals, so the gossip had it that he spent most of his time with another woman, or in and out of gaol.

Despite her sequestered lifestyle Ma Bacon was destined to influence her neighbours in a way that neither she nor they could have foreseen. Front-room windows of the houses in our road were arbitrarily furnished with white lace curtains, until the day when Ma's were re-hung dyed buff, or 'biscuit' as it was then fashionably termed. The neighbours were unanimous in condemnation: 'Who does she think she is? Just wanting to be different and making an exhibition of herself!' Yet, other biscuit-dyed curtains soon began to appear, house after house, until the road's front windows were transformed. If my mother had been asked how she and the others reconciled this with their former objection, I have no doubt that the reply would have been 'This is the way we do it now.'

Fashions are said to be fickle, which is certainly so when they are commercially manipulated, but changes of convention, popular habits or patterns of behaviour can be set in motion by unconscious pioneers like Ma Bacon. Such changes can take place so rapidly and completely as to obliterate public memory of what has been supplanted. Does anyone remember who was the first cricket umpire to officiate wearing a short white jacket in lieu of the hitherto obligatory long white coat extending below the knees? He must have felt embarrassingly conspicuous at first, but in due course his eccentricity came to be taken for granted as the conventional norm.

Accepted conventions can grow out of an apparent vacuum. For instance, it has become usual for church choirs, and often the congregations, to sing under the direction of a conductor. As a child I never saw or heard of this, and church services appeared to get by quite well without needing it.

A mass habit that has inexplicably changed over the years has been the substitution of 'um' for 'er' as the monosyllabic inter-jection between words in hesitant, thoughtful or laboured speech.

*

Two doors beyond Ma Bacon lived Mrs Cummings, whose hus-band was also away a great deal, but she was spared gossip because he was a cross-country telephone linesman and was nearly always at home at weekends and on public holidays. My mother referred to her as a 'respectable body', but treated her with some condescension because she was known to have been brought up in an orphanage. She had an elderly Pekinese bitch called Diddy who had a glass eye.

She spent every Monday at our house to do the family washing, which my mother claimed was far beyond her strength. It was indeed a strenuous task. The clothes boiler was coal-heated, and its copper bowl was set in a concrete base and had no tap, so that it needed to be baled out to empty it. After boiling, the wash was vigorously pummelled on a scrubbing board in the sink and then put through the mangle to squeeze out the surplus moisture before being hung out to dry. Throughout these stages Mrs Cummings would be singing Sankey and Moody hymns with frequent repetitions of her favourite, 'Throw out the lifeline, brother.'

Washing machine were far into the future. The only alternative to the laborious home wash was to send out to a laundry. These offered two grades of service: either so-called 'hand washing', which included ironing, with each item charged separately, or 'bag wash', charged by weight, with everything bundled together and returned unironed.

There were also the dry cleaners, then known as 'dyers and cleaners'. Dyestuffs had become very scarce during the war, and products for home dyeing did not reappear until several years later – indeed, Ma Bacon's lace curtains were the first things I heard mentioned as having been home 'dipped'. Some dyers and cleaners also undertook 'invisible' mending and promoted the service by practitioners at work seated in their shop windows. The first time I saw this I wanted to stop to watch what they were doing, but my mother said, 'Certainly not, it's rude to stare.' I protested that 'They're there to be seen working, aren't they?' 'Yes, but if we stand to watch them they'll look daggers back at us,' my mother insisted.

Mrs Cummings was also called in to help with the annual spring clean, although 'help' is hardly the appropriate word, as my mother would be exhausted to virtual inactivity on the day, having worked to a late hour overnight to ensure that the house was in a fit condition to be viewed beneath the surface by a neighbour. It would have been easier for my mother to have spread the task over a period, but the annual all-in-a-day ritual needed to be seen to be carried out. Balancing on the sharp edge between upper working class and lower middle class involved onerous responsibilities. I never heard my parents speak directly about class differences. When I first became aware of them it was merely that some people were said to be 'common' or 'ignorant', and were looked down upon, but that we looked up to those who were 'superior'.

Throughout my early childhood my mother tirelessly monitored my manners and speech to eradicate whatever she considered to be 'common'. Later, when I went on to grammar school, I had to conform to an added code of 'things that aren't done', among the first of which was that 'We don't clip pens or pencils in jacket outer pockets.' Many of the injunctions that followed stressed the vital importance of avoiding certain expressions, as for instance, 'Pleased to meet you!' and 'Pardon?' It was stressed that such solecisms provided an instant revelation of educational grounding, and during my adult life I have come across no evidence to contradict this judgement.

*

The Townsends lived almost opposite our house, but they were barely acknowledged until Mrs Townsend died from the Spanish flu and my mother undertook to look after her two young children for the day of her funeral. I had hardly spoken to them before, and I now learned that their father was a rent collector. This explained my mother's coolness towards the family, as she disapproved of rent collectors although living in rented property herself at that time.

During my early years the rent for our house was collected weekly by an elderly Dickensian character who entered each payment with a quill pen dipped into a non-spill ink bottle attached by a leather loop to a waistcoat button. The last time he called in the road he was accompanied by a new collector who was to succeed him on his retirement. His successor was introduced as a Mr Black, who was appropriately dressed in black with a long black cloak. Overhearing my mother telling my aunt that he was a 'new man' and that 'he hadn't a tooth in his head', I gained the childish impression that despite his grown-up stature he was newly born.

My mother's offer to care for the Townsend children for the day involved her in a shameful catastrophe. She had prepared cauliflower cheese with the midday meal, but when the elder child, Maudie, pushed her plate aside it was seen to harbour a caterpillar.

Mr Townsend soon engaged a live-in housekeeper, a widow he married after a respectable interval, whose arrival became the subject of prolonged speculation between my mother and Mrs Norris next door as to how old she might be. Age-guessing was one of their favourite pastimes. Face, hair and hands of a new acquaintance would be scrutinised intently, and possible clues revealed in conversation would be memorised and mulled-over. A direct question, however politely expressed, was unthinkable: one's age was personal private property. When my mother qualified to vote in 1927 she was dismayed to be required to state her age on the electoral registration form: '– and I thought the ballot was secret!' she protested.

Next door to the Townsends lived the Trubshaw couple and their teenage daughter Ruby. Mr Trubshaw was a newsagent and ran the neighbourhood newspaper delivery rounds. His shop kept no stock of periodicals, which were supplied only for regular orders. Every Wednesday morning with our *Daily Mail* came *Punch*, to be enjoyed during the weekend before my father took it off to his office, to be passed on to a colleague in the staff magazine club, of which each member contributed a different title for circulation among the others. It was due to this, later on, that I first read the Sherlock Holmes adventures when they appeared in the *Strand Magazine*.

The Trubshaws were keenly involved in amateur dramatics, and Mrs Trubshaw was prone to theatrical gestures and turns of speech. Gesticulation was minimal in everyday speech in those days, and my mother considered it 'quaint', which in her vocabulary almost equated with cranky. She modified this verdict in Mrs Trubshaw's case by adding, 'But, of course, she was brought up abroad, you know!' Whenever we stopped to speak with her when we were out she would grab me by the hand and pull me aside from my mother, explaining, 'This is the one I'm going to run off with!' This always alarmed me in case it might happen when I was alone – and the fear did indeed transpire to assume virtual reality. This came about one day when I was left in Ruby's charge at her house while our mothers went off for the day to the January sales in London's West End. My mother always came back exhausted from these expeditions, but she was sustained by her faith in Mrs Trubshaw's refined taste as a shopping companion, although with regret that she had 'married beneath her' to a shopkeeper.

As soon as the ladies left the house, Ruby said she would be upstairs for a while but would soon be back to make hot drinks for us. When the door opened again, however, there entered not Ruby but a stranger – a stooping, grey-haired old lady dressed in black, supporting herself with a stout stick. In dismay I cried out for Ruby. 'That'll do you no good,' said the old lady, scowling at me. 'I've done away with her, and now I'm going to run off with you!' As I screamed in terror she straightened up, relaxing her expression and casting off a wig, and I could see that she was Ruby dressed up in disguise. 'Only a little spruce,' she said. 'Just trying out the part I'm to play in our next show.'

'Sprucing' vulnerable young children was habitual then among many adults, but never, I am glad to recall, by my parents or any of my relatives. It often took the form of misinformation or exaggeration, told with a serious voice and facial expression, accompanied by a wink or a tapped nose to engage the complicity of other adults in the deception. Our next-door neighbour, Mr Norris, was an inveterate sprucer. Whenever he put a record on his gramophone, for instance, he would assure me that the music was played by a little man who lived inside the cabinet.

Further up the road towards its 'wrong' end (in my mother's estimation), we had few contacts beyond the Millwards. The exceptions were the Hyders and the Tottems. Mr Hyder was a storekeeper with an Irish wife and seven young children, including two sets of twins. Twice a year he and my father audited the accounts of the local cricket club, of which they were both playing members. Apart from that they seemed not to mix, except presumably at the club. Mr Tottem was a Civil Service clerk who had a son several years older than me. He and my father were on no more than nodding terms until the day when his employment at the War Office involved a dramatic train of local events, to be recounted in due course.

It was from Mr Tottem that my father acquired a mannerism of laughing that he practised habitually for many years. Laughter is a far from uniform human activity: it can vary from a barely vocalised titter or giggle to an exaggerated crescendo of explosive guffaws. In Mr Tottem's case – as adopted by my father – the loudly voiced element accompanied a histrionic hopping act, rotating on one leg so that his back was momentarily turned on whoever he was addressing, who might or might not be sharing his amusement.

*   *   *

The Spanish flu epidemic in 1918 affected our road less severely than some others nearby. There were three fatal cases: two of them, ironically, ex-servicemen who had survived long spells in the trenches. The initial indication of a death in the road, before word of mouth reached us, were the drawn daytime window blinds of the victim's house. In London's East End it was also the custom to spread straw across the road outside a house of mourning, to deaden the sound of hooves and iron-clad cart wheels on the cobbles. An outward display of bereavement was conventional custom during the 1920s: women would dress entirely in black, with a veil over the face, and men would wear black ties and armbands, for weeks, and often for months, after a funeral in the family.

The following year diphtheria was rampant, and the dreaded fever van was a frequent sight in the road. This was a larger-than-normal ambulance for highly infectious cases, in which the patient and all recently worn clothing and bedding were conveyed to an isolated fever hospital, the patient to languish there without visitors until recovery, or death. Any books on the premises were taken away to the municipal fumigation depot to be disinfected. They would probably be on loan from the public library, as Woodside residents – if our neighbours were representative – seemed rarely if ever to have books of their own.

The diphtheria epidemic coincided with a smallpox scare, and armbands of red ribbon worn by children indicated that they had recently been vaccinated. Parental refusal of vaccination required a medical certificate of grounds of conscientious objection, which then had to be sworn before a magistrate.

Our District Nurse, Miss Timms, pale-faced and care-worn, was engaged to marry Mr Bates, a burly countryman with a greengrocery shop in Brighton. My mother, who referred to her as 'a refined and genteel little person,' expressed misgivings about the marriage and predicted that she was destined to have to serve in the shop and live above it. When the wedding took place, however, it was announced that the bride would not be working and that the couple would reside in a new house built

17

for them in Hove. On a day trip to Brighton we called at the shop and found the new Mrs Bates, now bright-eyed and rosy-cheeked, cheerfully serving the customers. She told my parents that they were living over the premises since she had talked her husband into letting the new house to holiday visitors. My mother was convinced that her foreboding had been justified, but I felt sure she was mistaken. Children – or, at least, some of them – can sometimes sense beneath the surface more clearly than their elders.

*　　*　　*

If we turned left as we came out of our house – and my mother was never known to turn right – we came to Portland Road, the main thoroughfare leading to the High Street. If we crossed over to a side turning we reached Woodside Village, much older than the rest of Woodside, and indeed of all Norwood. Its extensive green, surrounded by venerable horse chestnut trees, was flanked by old cottages, some of them thatched, a few shops, and two public houses. The land behind the buildings along one side of the green was still farmed, and its farmhouse had a duck pond in its yard. Beyond the other side the farmland had been lost to a brickworks and the expansion of its clay pits. At the side of its former farmhouse was a farrier's forge, where we often paused to watch horses being shod. We would know from some distance away when shoeing was in progress from the ringing sounds of hammering on the anvil. It was a fine sight to see the sparks flying as the red-hot metal was battered into shape, and the clouds of hissing steam as the horseshoes were tried for size against the upturned hooves.

One of the village shops was our nearest greengrocery, and it was thanks to our regular custom there that I first tasted bananas, which had disappeared from sale, together with other tropical produce, during the war years. Oranges remained intermittently available, probably due to the shorter sea voyage from Spain. I was especially fond of bright red blood oranges, then commoner than latterly, which I persistently called 'bloody oranges', to my mother's horrified exasperation. She succeeded in eradicating my use of the *faux-pas* at home, but the shopkeeper conspired to keep it going by mischievously asking 'And what do you call this, then?' whenever he handed me one. My mother was eventually driven to change to another retailer.

A frequenter often to be seen on the Green was an eccentric character known as 'Paper Jack'. He was profusely bearded and abhorred textile garments, dressing himself instead with thick rolls of newspaper tied round his body. He was said to live in a crude shelter he had constructed at the brickworks. Many years later my mother sent me a reminiscent cutting from the local newspaper, after his death, in which his brother was quoted as saying that the family first realised that he was 'turning out odd' when he ceased shaving and gave up using towels, and preferred to run round the garden to get dry after his ablutions. Beards were rarely seen during my childhood, and were associated only with extreme old age or with a Bohemian lifestyle image. Moustaches, in contrast, were commonplace, and to be described as 'clean-shaven' implied a notable departure from normality. They were also an almost indispensable 'rite of passage' from teenage to adulthood.

In a nearby cottage lived our local chimney sweep, a dapper character, jaunty in manner, who drove a smart pony trap. In those days of almost total solid fuel consumption, sweeps were personages of some stature, and ours was popular and respected. Attendance at weddings by sweeps to greet the bride for luck was not customary in Woodside, or perhaps this supposedly ancient tradition had not yet been invented. Wedding dresses were much less elaborate than they were to become later, and were generally intended to become 'party wear' after the event. As much attention was devoted to the bride's 'going away' outfit to be worn during the honeymoon, and subsequently for special occasions, probably for many years to come.

The sweep's next-door neighbour was the knife grinder who plied in our road and was never short of custom as stainless cutlery was as yet far from in general use or popularly accepted. He was Irish, as most knife grinders were then, and I learnt later that they were reputed to stem from the Irish tinkers. Many years afterwards, in Paris, I encountered an Irish tinker busking with a pipe he claimed to have fashioned from silver refined from ore he had found in County Donegal. He asserted that his forebears long preceded the arrival of the Gypsies – with whom they are generally identified – and the Irish in Ireland. He also denied that Irish Roman Catholicism had been historically continuous. According to him, the Irish accepted the Reformation as readily as the English but recanted when persuaded by Jesuit missionaries that allegiance to Rome would be seen as a political gesture against the English crown.

A shoe repairer shared the knife grinder's cottage and worked at his bench in its front room. Shoe repairers were known as 'snobs', and their craft as 'snobbing', locally and perhaps much further afield. I never heard them called cobblers. This one was a retired brewery cooper, and my father explained to me that a 'wet' cooper's work was highly skilled, as his barrels needed to be leak-proof, whereas those of a 'dry' cooper held only solid produce such as apples.

The next door premises had a conservatory in front, and this was the village barbershop. Its proprietor was the regularly defeated candidate of the Labour Party at elections in our constituency, and my parents always referred to him as 'a red-hot socialist', but then I never heard tell from them of socialists of any other temperature. My interest in his shop was centred on a magnificent stuffed pike in a glass case that had been caught, so I was told, in one of the lakes in the Crystal Palace grounds.

Our first window cleaner I can recall was a Woodside villager, but before long he went absent to serve a gaol sentence, as did his successor soon after. Indeed, a tendency to incur imprisonment seemed to be an occupational hazard of the trade in those times. Another short-lived cleaner had a pair of whippets I greatly admired, and was said to augment his income by poaching rabbits on the Council-owned farmland opposite the lower end of our road.

The chimney sweep, the knife grinder, and the window cleaner all had to be dealt with at the street door, but my mother disapproved strongly of making purchases there, which she considered 'common'. We had a metal plate attached to the front gate warning 'No Hawkers, Canvassers, or Circulars', but it was far from effective. If there had been a kitchen door that was accessible to tradesmen, she would doubtless have felt that it was appropriate to deal with them there. She never entirely adjusted to the limitations of dwelling in a terrace house, even though born and bred in one.

21

An exception to her prejudice against hawkers at the door was the itinerant French onion seller, who arrived regularly in late autumn. She was firmly convinced of the superior quality of these onions, as were both my grandmothers, and as they had bought them throughout their housewife years the traffic was evidently long established. The onion seller who served our road seemed to have just about enough command of English to carry out his transactions, but I once overheard him engaged in a more sustained conversation with the local dairyman's wife. She came from Aberystwyth and spoke Welsh with her family. My Uncle Joe was with me at the time and said that the man's speech was in the Breton language, which he had heard spoken during his wartime service in Brittany.

One of the village shopkeepers was the herbalist Prothero, who described himself as a 'therapeutic botanist'. We went there sometimes for a purgative called ipecacuanha wine, and syrup of squills, a cough remedy said to be derived from the shoreside sea onion. I found them both unpleasant, but the glamour of their names provided some compensation. My mother also bought there a powder called Salanaise, that when mixed with milk made a delicious salad dressing. This was years before anything similar came on sale in jars.

Mr Prothero was a softly-spoken young man who habitually wore shantung shirts with soft collars, a noticeable eccentricity for a tradesman then. He lived with two aunts, both retired nurses, over the shop, and they were said to be Theosophists and vegetarians. My mother was once invited there for an evening meal, and came back to recount her dismay when offered cabbage water to drink with it.

*   *   *

Most of our household shopping was in Portland Road, upwards of a mile in length and lined intermittently with shops. There were also the parish church and several chapels, a Salvation Army citadel, two small, scruffy cinemas, and five public houses. In a yard at the back of one of them, as I overheard a neighbour telling my father, the ancient game of quoits was still played. This involved heavy iron rings thrown to encircle pegs protruding from a dampened clay bed. Its apparent simplicity was bedevilled by a complexity of rules, often subjected to disputes. On at least one occasion players were said to have been arrested for assaulting the umpire.

The shops varied in evidence of prosperity or lack of it. Perhaps as an effect of wartime and postwar pressures on downmarket economy, some of the retail premises were divided into two, with separate doors in the original entrance space, and some pairs of these half-shops had reverted to whole-shop status. Then there were some house-shops – converted residential premises – and shop-houses, the reverse conversion.

In one of the house-shops was the office of Foster's removals and storage firm, with its yard and stables at the rear. Here we always paused to admire the fascia board with its fine lettering painted by my Grandfather Silverwood. He had also painted their pantechnicon, the company name backed by a scenic representation of removals by road, rail and sea. He was a talented craftsman and artist, a countryman by disposition, born and bred in Kent, but his entire adult life was spent in London's East End.

East London, from Aldgate for more than a mile along Whitechapel and the Mile End Road, was then an immigrant Jewish settlement, mostly from Eastern Europe. Shopfront fascias and posters were monopolised by Hebrew lettering, there were Yiddish language theatres and cinemas, kosher restaurants, and synagogues abounded. Scattered enclaves of non-Jewish residents in Stepney, Bethnal Green and Bromley-by-Bow could be likened to Christian ghettos.

Oddly, as it now seems in retrospect, my parents told me

23

nothing about Jews, and I never heard them refer to them, although born and bred in predominantly Jewish surroundings. Apart from the Bible, my Uncle Wally was my only source of information on the subject as a child. During the war he served with many Jews in a locally recruited regiment, and had acquired a taste for some of their ethnic dishes. Several times he took me to Bloom's kosher restaurant in Whitechapel and explained to me the elements of their dietary laws, which proved useful in later life when on visits to New York, and while I was living in Jerusalem.

*

Grandfather Silverwood was mild-mannered and quietly spoken, and only once I heard his voice raised in anger: when my Aunt Rene said she was thinking about getting her hair bobbed. 'If your hair's cut off, I'll break up the home!' he threatened. I failed to understand that this implied abandoning the family, and I imagined him smashing up the furniture with a sledgehammer. Looking back, it seems illogical that feminine fashions for short hair waited until the 1920s: they would surely have been more convenient during the war, when countless numbers of women were working in factories and hospitals and on the land.

Grandfather Silverwood's two brothers, my Great-uncles Tom and Alec, were more adventurous. Tom was a world-wide wanderer who made and lost several small fortunes prospecting for gold and precious stones. He came back briefly on rare visits between expeditions, to the Yukon after gold, Burma for rubies, Australia for opals, Brazil for emeralds. He seems to have been intermittently successful but to have lacked the persistence to exploit his opportunities. I remember him on one visit spilling out the contents of a bag of stones from which my grandmother, my mother and aunts could take their pick, to be cut and mounted at his expense. Then he was off again, bound for Australia, although he disembarked at Cape Town to look up an acquaintance in the diamond trade, and missed the vessel's departure.

Great-uncle Alec settled in Shanghai and became manager of the waterworks there. His marriage to a Japanese lady aroused some family consternation, and politely veiled relief was evident when news of her death arrived. The relief was premature, however: he subsequently married her sister.

*

Five adjoining food shops in Portland Road were owned and operated by a highly distinctive religious sect of which the adherents called themselves The Body of Dependants, founded in 1850 by John Sirgood, a dissident from The Plumstead Peculiars. They were locally known as Cokelers, a reference to their preference for cocoa, as they abhorred tea, coffee and alcoholic beverages. They lived communally over the shops, and men and women dressed in mid-Victorian clothes, changing fashions having been disregarded ever since the community's foundation. They disapproved of marriage: if members did marry, they were excluded from the community for three years before they could be re-admitted. Death was celebrated joyously, the coffin accompanied on foot all the way to the cemetery by the entire community singing, and garlanded with flowers. They were popular locally as they showed no disapproval of non-believers and made no effort to gain converts.

My mother's cousin, Lily Silverwood, was a member of the community for several years. She was eclectic in her quest for spiritual enlightenment. At an early age she had been converted by Mormon missionaries during the period when their church still practised polygamy, but she became disillusioned when her wish to emigrate to Salt Lake City was denied. After

25

leaving the Cokelers she joined the New and Latter House of Israel, commonly called the Jezreelites, but ended her life as a Strict and Particular Baptist after a brief interlude with the Seventh Day Adventists. Her small estate was bequeathed to the Lord's Day Observance Society, subject to her executors being convinced that the Lord's Day was Sunday and not Saturday as Biblically ordained, failing which the Cats' Protection League would be the beneficiary. The executors were my father and the solicitor who drafted her will. After several meetings with the Society's officials they remained sceptical, to the advantage of the felines.

The Jezreelites were the most eccentrically heterodox of the many minor religious sects whose literature I have collected during my adult years. An offshoot of the eighteenth-century 'visitation' of the prophetess Joanna Southcott, their doctrine was nominally Christian but involved Judaic elements, such as a Book of the Law that governed their daily lives in minutest detail. By the observance of its rules they held that the physical immortality of the 144,000 'elect' would be assured. That deaths continued was seen as evidence that the tenets of the Law had not been observed with adequate zeal. In common with several other sects deriving from the Southcott 'visitation' they believed that her sealed box contained divinely inspired messages that would herald a new age and provide solutions to the world's problems. Her detailed instructions as to the ritual opening of the box required the presence of 24 bishops, but their attendance is still awaited.

Similarly to the Cokelers, the Jezreelites established retail businesses to support their faithful. At their centre at Chatham in Kent they began the construction of a tower, never completed, that was intended to reach to heaven. Only a remnant of the sect survives in England at the end of the century, but still advertises regularly in *Old Moore's Almanac*.

*

26

One of my favourite shops in Portland Road was a corn chandlers, where newly hatched chicks were often displayed in the window. This was a branch of the Sanders Brothers chain, long ago closed in Britain but continuing for many more years in Belgium, where I learnt that it began, and also that Sanders was a commonplace Belgian name. This reminds that when I was living in Jerusalem my landlord was an immigrant from Poland whose name was Robinson. He denied any English connections and assured me that Robinson was a venerable old Polish name. Since then I have no longer doubted the authenticity of the Swiss Family Robinson.

Another 'out-of-place' Robinson is the woody Paris suburb of that name, formerly reputed for its cafés built into the branches of trees, and so described in English language guides, published as so-called revised editions until recent times. Visitors guided by them who went in search of the tree-top retreats were destined to disappointment: they finally ceased to trade in 1914.

Next door to Sanders Brothers was our nearest Post Office, as drab and bare as they came in those days. Apart from its counter service it offered for sale only a meagre assortment of writing pads, envelopes and plain postcards, but surprisingly there were also toy-size wooden wheelbarrows displayed for sale in its otherwise bare window.

Sait's Dairy, across the road, dealt only in milk, cream, butter, and eggs. This was usual at that time, as the odour of cheese was thought to endanger the freshness of the unpasteurised milk. If cheese was required, one went to a grocer who was also a provision merchant – some were not and stocked only 'dry goods'.

A glass of milk could be enjoyed on the premises, seated at a marble-topped table in the window, and perhaps with a sponge cake, of which a stock was kept under a bell-glass on the counter. Why only sponge cakes I never knew, but they were the standard accompaniment of milk consumed on dairy premises in those days.

Butter from a vast mound was served into individual portions with a pair of wooden patters embossed with the dairy's name.

Eggs were piled in a basket, mingled with odd bits of straw, left doubtless as evidence that they were freshly gathered. There was usually a choice of white or tinted shells, and sometimes brown, often speckled. My mother was convinced that the more pigmented the shell the more nutritious the content, but many people then held that a white shell was an indication of purity. In fact, as I learnt long afterwards, shell colour is inherited independently of content quality. Another fallacy widespread at that time was that white-shelled eggs were laid only by hens with white plumage. Yet another fallacy, still current, is that yellow-shanked fowl have been cornfed, although shank colour derives from parentage alone.

Some dairies still kept cows in stalls behind their shops, but Sait's cows were housed in nearby Albert Road, as I was to discover when my grandmother took me there.

Our milkman, who delivered twice daily, came from Sait's. His brightly-painted horse-drawn float reminded me of a picture of Queen Boadicea's chariot. It bore an urn with a tap from which a bucket was replenished to convey the milk to the doorstep, to be ladled into the housewife's jug. For the early delivery, around 7 a.m., the jug was left at the door, covered by a pudding basin to protect its contents from cats and birds.

Sait's closed down while I was still a schoolboy, penalised, so it was said, by a Ministry requirement to install a refrigeration plant that the owner claimed he had never needed, and in any event was beyond his means.

Refrigeration then was largely restricted to cold stores in wholesale meat warehouses and some few larger retail butcheries. Cold display units in shops, and household refrigerators were far into the future and awaited the more general availability of electricity. Most houses in Woodside were gas-lit until the early 1930s, and some of the older properties were still dependent on oil lamps. The local gas company was still promoting its lighting service as late as 1928, when its newly built showroom in the High Street was entirely gas-lighted. Street lamps were all gas in Woodside throughout the 1920s, and were

28

turned on and off around dusk and dawn by men who went round with long poles.

Milk was not the only twice-daily household delivery then: the baker's roundsman called early and around midday. The butcher's boy called every morning for orders, with which he would return promptly if they were for a midday meal. Rival butcher's boys driving their light two-wheeled gigs drawn by high-stepping Hackney ponies were often involved in perilous racing contests on the public thoroughfares.

My father was insistent that these services would never discontinue 'because the public wouldn't stand for it'. He was prone to such dogmatic pronouncements. When set bus stops first appeared in the London area in the early 1930s with signs requiring 'queue this side', he protested that 'we English will never queue for anything, it's against the national character.' He lived until English queues had become proverbial abroad, but if reminded of a failed past dictum he would deny it strenuously, and if pressed, angrily.

*

An authentic period survival among the Portland Road shops was the Workmen's Dining Room, with high-backed benches and tables set in rows on either side of a gangway leading to the serving hatch. Breakfast 'fry-ups' were served all day from an early hour, and roast dinners ('cut from the joint and two veg') during the middle of the day. Such establishments, categorised as 'good pull-ups for carmen', were formerly widespread throughout the London area, but they were dwindling rapidly in number by the early years of the 1930s.

Facilities for eating out were severely limited during this period. Fish and chips were strictly 'takeaway', public houses were foodless, and even the buffet at Norwood Junction station offered only sandwiches (a choice of ham or cheese) and meat pies, all of doubtful freshness. For a light snack there was only the dairy offering of a sponge cake with a glass of milk, or the jellied eel stall in the Saturday street market.

Restaurants and hotels serving meals to non-residents were few in number around South London, and were confined to town centres. Oddly, in contrast the nearby countryside within walking distance of our house had numerous wayside cottages with signboards announcing 'Teas, Light Refreshments and Minerals', many of them accredited by the Cyclists' Touring Club. 'Teas with Hovis' was another familiar country sign.

The popular Lyons teashops – the nearest was in central Croydon – served cooked meals and snacks throughout the day, and during the 1920s its waitresses still wore Victorian parlour-maid uniform. Soon after I first attended school in Croydon, the Lyons there introduced an 'American soda fountain' serving fruit-flavoured beverages and ice-cream treats.

In central London and many towns in the South, but not in Croydon, several chains competed with Lyons, notably ABC (short for Aerated Bread Company), Express Dairy, and Pearce and Plenty. The latter's shops featured separate entry and exit doors faced with distorting mirrors. On the way in, one's image was meagrely thin and grey, but on the way out it had become plump and pink. My mother ruled out ABC teashops after over-hearing two ladies in conversation at a nearby table in one of them. One ordered a cooked dish, the other only a cup of tea, commenting, 'I couldn't possibly eat here: I used to be man-ageress of one of these, and I know what the conditions are like in their kitchens.' Unlike their rivals, ABC teashops provided accommodation upstairs for 'ladies only'.

The catering scene at the seaside holiday resorts was very different from that of either central London or its suburbs. There were cafés in profusion, since the majority of holidaymakers stayed in boarding houses or bed-and-breakfast accommodation providing no midday or evening meals. Indeed, many of them in those days locked their doors on their boarders once breakfast had been taken. Some that permitted later meals to be brought in to be consumed in their dining rooms levied a charge 'for the use of the cruet'.

Those who, like my parents, preferred less regimented accommodation, stayed in 'board and lodgings', which were private houses receiving one couple or a small family in a down-stairs sitting/dining room and one or more bedrooms. The addresses of approved establishments were passed between rela-tives and friends with confidential discretion. A phrase I often overheard when these recommended holiday bookings were under discussion was 'just plain cooking, you know', in a tone of voice between praiseworthy and deprecatory. I later came to realise that this expression conveyed the coded message 'but don't expect home-baked cakes'.

Our seaside holidays for several years after the war were spent at Bognor, later to be dignified as Bognor Regis in honour of its connections with King George V. The climate at Bognor was claimed to be 'bracing', whereas at Littlehampton, only a few miles along the coast, it was said to be 'relaxing'. When I first remember it – I think it would have been in 1920 – Bognor still preserved some of the elements of pre-war coastal resorts. Wicker Bath chairs, popularised by Queen Victoria in her later years, still plied for hire on the promenade, and along the beach were ranged bathing machines – oddly so-named, as there was nothing mechanical about them. They were just bathing huts mounted on large cartwheels, enabling bathers to be horse-drawn to the sea, which at low tide could be a consider-able distance away.

Old timbered groynes built out from the promenade across the beach attracted a harvest of whelks, of which my Grandfather Silverwood was particularly fond. He would come down for a day while we were there, and the sight of him swal-lowing whelks, his Adam's apple rising and falling at each gulp, prejudiced me against any kind of shellfish for the rest of my life.

On the sands when the tide was out there were children's rides on donkeys and the pitch of the Punch and Judy

31

'Professor', as all the members of his calling were then styled. Looking down from the promenade we might pause to admire the sand sculptor's painstaking but transient art, doomed to be obliterated at the next high tide. At the pier's end a small theatre provided concert party entertainment, its performers clad in Pierrot costumes of loose white tunics with ruffed collars and conical white hats. For a while I thought that a Pierrot was so-called because he acted on a pier, until my Aunt May told me that it was the name of a stock character in the traditional Harlequinade that preceded the seasonal pantomimes.

The first pantomime I was taken to was *Cinderella*, at the Queen's Music-hall in Poplar while we were staying with my Silverwood grandparents over Christmas. Cinder's coach to take her to the ball was drawn by a team of six Shetland ponies, but I was firmly convinced that they were really large dogs. The following season we were the guests of our neighbour Mrs Trubshaw, seated in a box with some of her fellow members of the Norwood Amateur Dramatic Society. The production that year was *Humpty Dumpty*, but to my disappointment it involved neither ponies nor dogs, nor any other livestock.

*   *   *

The parish church in Portland Road had a popular Sunday school, of which my father was superintendent for some years until he was summarily dismissed by a change of vicar on the grounds of wearing cassock and surplice 'without canonical authority' while officiating. His consequent embitterment was emphasised by the manner of his dismissal: the vicar sent his verger to deliver it.

The previous incumbent had been vicar of the East End parish where my parents lived before their marriage, and he became my godfather. He was a large, easy-going Scot who was never known to express any religious opinions outside his sermons, and they were also comfortingly non-committal. One of his former curates became an archdeacon in a northern diocese and used to stay with my parents when attending Convocation. Garbed in tailcoat, gaiters, and top hat, his coming and going within view of our neighbours doubtless gave my mother immense satisfaction.

After his loss of office at our local church, my father joined the congregation of an Anglican church in central Croydon. The vicar there was a former Quaker, a descendent of Elizabeth Fry, the Victorian prison reformer. His services were 'low church' to its extreme. His lengthy extempore prayers were delivered on his knees at the rear of the congregation, and he celebrated Communion (here termed 'the Lord's Supper', but to my father 'early service') at a 'holy table' with his back to the altar, long before this was generally adopted. These services were virtually indistinguishable from 'chapel', but they suited my father, who attended them regularly for many years. This seems to have conflicted with his distaste for nonconformity and opposition to disestablishment, then widely mooted. During lengthy – and sometimes acrimonious – discussions on the subject with my Uncle Wally, his brother-in-law, his expression would take on its gravest aspect, with the corners of his mouth drawn down severely. This was a facial mannerism he derived, I think, from newspaper illustrations of Mr Justice Avory, a notoriously harsh judge he greatly admired. Dogmatic statements would be delivered with closed eyes, to emphasise that he was not prepared to see them contradicted, I presume. He was addicted, during serious discussions, to the expression 'as a matter of fact', often applied in contexts that were far from factual. Later on, influenced by a solicitor who worked at his office, he switched to the prevalent legal version 'in point of fact'.

My father was a Civil Servant throughout his career, starting as a messenger boy and rising to middle rank while daydreaming of alternative occupations that might have been. The clergy was among several of these, which also included the law, accountancy, and schoolmastering. During each phase he adopted something of the characteristics of the wishful role, and I guess that his cassock-and-surplice period was the closest he got to any of them.

I was not allowed to attend his Sunday school as I might mix with rough children there, my mother decided. The same risk was ascribed to the refusal to let me join the Scouts. For this, my father had an additional reason. As a young man, he had been out walking in the country when a balloon made a forced descent. A scoutmaster whistled up his troop to form a cordon around it to ensure its safety, and my father for ever after denounced his 'officious behaviour', and vowed that no child of his would be subjected to such an influence.

The house next to the Vicarage had a brass plate on its gate, announcing that it was occupied by a dentist. This drew a disparaging comment from my father whenever we passed it: 'You see, no letters after his name – the man's a quack!' I should explain that dentists at that time were free to practise without formal qualifications. Professional 'letters after names' were conspicuously displayed in those days: every dispensing chemist, for instance, added MPS (to denote Membership of the Pharmaceutical Society) after his or her name above the shop. For a long time my mother was convinced that every MPS 'knew Latin', until one of them admitted to her that his knowledge of the language was only adequate to deal with medical prescriptions.

A garage opposite the church was the first in the district to install a petrol pump. Operated manually by means of a crank handle, it delivered Pratt's Perfection Spirit, later to be renamed Esso. Until then, petrol was supplied only in cans to be poured into the vehicle tanks. This garage held the local agency for the Scott Sociable three-wheeler, and briefly for the earliest motor scooters, until they were banned from the roads as too dangerous to riders and other traffic.

The Scott Sociable had a single front wheel on the offside and a chassis of motorcycle and sidecar plan, although the bodywork of both elements was integrated. All those displayed on the forecourt, and every one I ever saw on the road, were coloured mauve, or as my father preferred to call it, 'episcopal purple'. This was a distinctive feature at a time when there was sparse choice of colour for vehicle coachwork, and the creator of the ubiquitous Model T Ford was said to have decreed 'They can have any colour they want, so long as it's black.' His other often-quoted dictum, 'History is bunk', was confounded after his demise by the opening of a museum bearing his name devoted to the history of the United States. Motorcycles were almost always black, the exception being the maroon-coloured Indian. I only saw black pedal cycles, although my mother recalled owning a green one, but that had been before the war.

The currency of the Scott Sociable was quite brief, perhaps because it accommodated only a single passenger, whereas the conventional motorcycle and sidecar, with which it competed, could take another riding pillion. The popular three-wheeler of the time was the Morgan, with two wheels in front, and almost solely a passenger carrier in England. In France, however, similar vehicles with load-carrying bodies were (and still are) widely used by local tradesmen. They are especially associated with coal and wine delivery, often on the same vehicle, as the two commodities have close commercial links there. When I first lived in Paris in the 1930s, many coal merchants took orders for wines to be delivered, and supplied wine by the glass for consumption on their premises.

Limited protection from adverse weather may have been the main disadvantage of the Morgan in this country. The significant breakthrough for popular family motoring was the advent of the Austin Seven in 1922. This provided low-price saloon car conditions with economical running cost and touring capability, as distinct from local 'runabout' motoring. Its success was immediate, and countless couples and families took to the roads for the first time, with no driving test in force to delay them.

The main competitor to the Austin for a few years was the Trojan, built in Croydon. This had a two-stroke engine claimed to have only seven moving parts, a spartan interior, and solid-tyred wheels that were apt to get trapped in the tram lines.

*   *   *

As a shopping venue Portland Road was far from flourishing, but the Saturday street market along its upper length was always thronged until late in the evening, long after the shops closed, its stalls lighted by naphthalene flares in winter. They provided fruit and vegetables, domestic goods and hardware of all kinds, and some unclassifiable miscellaneous merchandise. There was regularly a quack 'professor' who peddled pills guaranteed to alleviate indigestion, and that could also be dissolved in a foot-bath of warm water to eliminate corns. His glib pseudo-scientific patter was enhanced by the presence of a live snake on his stall to exemplify his claim that the same pills were an infallible remedy for snake bite.

One of my favourite stalls displayed a stuffed badger and was devoted to the sale of badger's grease, claimed to be a sovereign treatment for baldness. The strongly smelling unguent was packed in old stone jam jars covered with canvas squares held fast by rubber bands. Baldness was much less prevalent then than it has become since. Grandfather Hutchings was severely bald and hopefully applied badger's grease to his pate night and morning, but without apparent benefit. His hair growth was restricted to meagre white fringes above each ear, although he retained incongrously dark bushy eyebrows to the end of his days.

Another stall announced that its proprietor was 'Hairdresser to the Thespians'. His stock-in-trade was a hair-curling lotion applied in sachets attached to hanks of hair by rubber bands. He promoted his product by inviting ladies attracted by his spiel to be the subjects of demonstration, seated on the stall. Once when we were returning home by bus past his stall, I saw him press something into the hand of his model, who recoiled with an expression of the utmost horror. Whatever could it have been? Regular home hair-curling was performed with curling tongs and a crimping iron heated in a candle flame. Professional 'permanent waving' was unknown: there were no ladies' hairdressing salons locally, and 'home perms' were still far into the future.

The pony-drawn sarsaparilla wagon was fashioned in the form of a barrel. A host of health-promoting properties were claimed for this exotic beverage by its stetson-hatted purveyor, but I was strictly forbidden it by my mother. Long afterwards, as an adult, I sampled it from a street vendor in New York and found that it resembled modern cola drinks in appearance and taste.

Our family butcher had a Saturday stall outside his shop to display Sunday joints, tended by an assistant clad in blue-and-white striped overalls, with a sharpening iron hanging from his belt like a sword. 'Come buy, buy, buy' was his incessant cry between serving customers. The joints would be almost exclusively beef or mutton, to be boiled as often as roasted. Lamb was a rarity, except in the form of chops, and veal I never heard mentioned. Mutton was as popular as beef, and I cannot understand its virtual disappearance in modern times – at least, in England, as it is still appreciated in Scotland and Wales. For pork my mother always went to another shop, a specialist pork butcher who sold joints and chops and pork sausages, but not bacon. Oddly, as it now seems, he also stocked tripe, although by definition it derives only from ruminants – cattle and sheep – and not from pigs.

A picturesque figure often seen strolling among the Saturday shoppers was popularly known as 'Christmas Tree Jack'. He dressed in a pale tussore suit with ornate epaulettes and a white cap with a gilded peak. It was said that as a bridegroom he was jilted at the altar and had made a vow to wear his wedding costume in perpetuity in memory of his lost bride. If he was suffering from a broken heart he showed no other evidence of it, as he was always benign and jovial whenever I saw him. I wondered why the 'Christmas' epithet in the absence of any Yule-like attributes. 'Jack' was readily understood, as it was applied by my mother, and many of her generation, to anyone who deviated from conventional conformity to become a crank. By her reckoning I qualified as a crank when, in my teens, I gave up the daily struggle to part my hair and swept it back unparted, and again when I decided to wear my trousers without turn-ups. My father's equivalent word was 'maniac', used chiefly in religious contexts, and applied especially to street preachers, then known as 'Bible thumpers'. He was apt to express intolerance of any show of enthusiasm in the name of religion, and it has since occurred to me to wonder why he never expressed any disapproval of my mother's cousin Lily's varied church allegiancies.

Another eccentric character – this one spared the 'Jack' epithet – often mingling with the street market shoppers, was known as 'the Baron'. He was said to be a Portuguese royalist living in exile since the republican revolution there before the war. During the summer he wore a straw boater hat in which a flap, propped open with a toothpick, had been cut in the crown for ventilation. In winter he often inconveniently carried a pair of skis on his shoulder. I once overhead him telling someone that the Lapps of northern Finland were the only people on earth who recognised no god and had no religion.

The upper end of Portland Road terminated at the railway bridge bearing trains to nearby Norwood Junction station and on to London and the South Coast. Seated on a campstool at the kerbside under the bridge, there was often an aged hawker of tea cosies, evidently home-made from scraps in patchwork fashion. His features were obscured by an overgrown beard, and his knitted headgear was always pulled down over his ears and forehead. From the first time I saw him I felt certain that he was a dog dressed in human clothing. I secretly retained this conviction (and another, that all dogs were males, and cats females) until well after I was old enough to have outgrown such childish fantasies.

*   *   *

39

On the other side of the bridge was the foot of South Norwood Hill, a prosperous area of large detached houses in extensive grounds. Turning left or right was the High Street, a shopping centre of much higher pretensions than Portland Road. Among its proudest emporia was Gale's, the drapers, haberdashers and costumiers, with an extended frontage of brass-framed windows reaching almost to pavement level. During the Christmas season one of these windows would display a large decorative model devised from pinned handkerchiefs – I recall an aeroplane, a locomotive, and the airship R34 in successive years.

Gale's emulated the superior manners of metropolitan trade. A gentlemanly 'shopwalker', clad in frock coat, cravat and spats, hovered at the entrance to greet each customer and enquire her wishes. A young lady assistant would then be summoned ('Forward, Miss Jones!') to escort the customer to the appropriate counter, each of which was furnished with very high-legged cane-seated chairs. At the back of the shop an elderly lady cashier presided at an elevated desk resembling a pulpit, from which a network of overhead wires connected to each counter. Along these wires sped payments and change borne in canisters dispatched by spring-loaded handles.

The serving assistants were trained to refined speech and genteel turns of phrase. I recall overhearing examples such as 'This style also comes in pink, modom', and 'Would there be anything in a blouse today, modom?' They were said to reside in the attics above the shop and to be subject to strict routines, allowed out only on early-closing day and on Sunday afternoon, provided that they attended church or chapel in the morning. This information came from my mother's Cousin Lily and may have been outdated, as she had worked there many years before, straight from school.

When Cousin Lily left Gale's she entered domestic service with a Miss Elgin in Lewisham, in a large house employing a cook-housekeeper and several housemaids and kitchenmaids. My only recollection of Miss Elgin is on visits, when my mother was entertained in the kitchen and I was left in the drawing

40

room with the lady of the house and required to play the board game called Halma, at which she cheated absent-mindedly.

I was spared this ordeal on one visit, when a boy of my own age had been invited 'to be my little friend'. His name was Raymond, he wore a green corduroy suit, and we shared a mutual dislike on sight. We were sent out to play in the back garden, which was dankly overgrown with ferns and nothing else, where we speechlessly nursed our animosity until called in to afternoon tea.

Cousin Lily eventually progressed to the status of house-keeper-companion, and in due course became one of Miss Elgin's legatees on her decease. The house was lavishly furnished and she inherited its entire contents, but the freehold remained with trustees who required rent for its occupation. She struggled 'to keep the home together', as she interpreted the late mistress's wishes, and a succession of 'paying guests' propped up a relentlessly losing battle.

It was during this period that Cousin Lily aspired to emigrate to Salt Lake City, but it seems that visiting Mormon dignitaries found the hospitality she provided them indispensable to the divine purpose. Her disillusionment asserted itself by the time she was forced to sell off her inheritance, and that was when she sought refuge with the Cokelers.

*

Lipton's High Street grocery and provision store was infinitely superior to any in Portland Road, and would have been entirely out of place had it have been sited there. The Royal Arms above the entrance testified the company's Appointment to their Majesties. The branch manager was a Licensed Dealer in Game, and a prominent notice announced that Families May be Waited upon Daily. Game was not alone in being restricted to licensed dealers: retailers then also needed licences to sell

41

postage stamps, playing cards and Church of England Prayer Books.

My mother was persuaded to make purchases there by Aunt May when they shopped in the High Street together, because when her mother was in service the family always patronised the local Lipton's, except when in Town for the Season, when it would be Fortnum and Mason, of course. My aunt's advocacy was underlined when one day we saw a landau drawn up outside the shop and the manager taking down an order from its passenger, while the coachman stood by the horse. 'That will be one of the ladies from South Norwood Hill attending to the household shopping in person, as the weather is so clement today,' said my aunt. My mother conceded the superiority of Lipton's products with one exception: she remained faithful to Typhoo tea because it was then sold only in pharmacies, which convinced her of its health-giving benefit.

I was fascinated by Lipton's coffee-roasting machine of revolving cylinders over a gas-heated bed. After roasting the coffee beans were ground and weighed to order and wrapped in a stiff paper cone, deftly rolled with the point securely twisted and the top corner flap tucked in. This mode of wrapping was also used for other loose dry goods such as tea, cocoa, sugar and rice. The assistant attending to coffee roasting at Lipton's wore a hand-folded paper hat in the style of a serviceman's forage cap. Later in life when I was working in Fleet Street, I found that headgear similarly folded was customarily worn on duty by newspaper press operatives.

Opposite Lipton's was the sweet shop of Clark, Nichols and Coombes. This firm operated a retail chain and manufactured confectionery under the brand name 'Clarnico'. The manageress of our branch affected an outdated fashion phase deriving from the Anglo-Japanese Exhibition at Earl's Court in 1910: she wore her hair piled high, her face was whitely powdered, and her dresses were in kimono style.

The shops and the products disappeared during the Second World War, but later I stumbled across the firm's name in the

London Telephone Directory. Curiosity tempted me to ring the number and enquire the fate of their products. The answer was that instead of sweetmeats they now supplied equipment for others to make them. Few sweets appealed to me as a child, but I was addicted to Clarnico marzipan bars, and then or since I have never known any other marzipan to equal theirs. The only taste with which it can compare is the French *sirop d'orgeat*, an almond concentrate used for mixing children's beverages and cocktails.

When I was first at school, the current sweet preference was for gobstoppers. These were large balls – inconveniently large for many small mouths – sickly sweet and peppermint flavoured. Their appeal was not primarily the taste but their constant changes as they were sucked, layer after layer revealing a different colour. I disliked them intensely, not only for their flavour but for the sticky fingers resulting from the frequent need to take them from the mouth to witness the various transformations.

Clarnico marzipan and all chocolate and candy bars were sold unwrapped when I first went to school. As wrapping was gradually introduced it seemed like a modern innovation, but I have since realised that its absence stemmed from wartime economy and that sophisticated packaging had been developed long previously. Children who grew up during and soon after the Second World War probably experienced a similar misconception.

*

Whenever I went to the High Street with my father or one of my grandfathers, we stopped at Hardham's the tobacconist. At the doorway stood a life-size effigy of a Red Indian in feathered head-dress, smoking his pipe of peace. This elaborate trade symbol was secured to the doorpost by a padlocked chain, but the proprietor would release it to the custody of the local rugby team when playing home games, as they had adopted it as their mascot. On one occasion it was seized on its way to the ground by supporters of the rival team, and held to ransom. The home team had to pay up, as otherwise they would have forfeited the deposit left with the tobacconist to ensure its safe return.

Hardham's window display always held my attention, which was fortunate, as I often had to wait there quite some time while serious discussion took place inside with the proprietor. At the front were samples of loose pipe tobaccos, with exotic-sounding names like Latakia, Montalk and Malabar, and tins of proprietary brands such as Balkan Sobranie and Saint Bruno, the latter the preference of both my grandfathers. Pipe-smoking was prevalent among men of all ages, and was seen as a significant step from adolescence to adult manhood. As a centre-piece was a pile of Mariner's Plug in bars wrapped in hessian, bound with twine. Behind were racks of pipes of all shapes and sizes. On one side were boxes of cigars and cheroots, and the other side was devoted to cigarettes. The most popular brands of the time were Player's Navy Cut and Wills' Gold Flake, and also displayed were Abdullah, De Reske, Passing Clouds and Churchman's, my father's favourite. Cigarettes were also sold loose, a choice of Virginian, Turkish, Egyptian or Russian.

As a smoker my father was unadventurous, but he was fond of mentioning that he had enjoyed French cigarettes during his time across the Channel. This 'time' was in fact a day trip to Boulogne while on holiday in Folkestone in 1912, but he came back from it an authority on everything French, and later in my life, after I had lived in France for some years, he was still informing me on the subject of French habits and customs. Apart from snide remarks about snails and frogs' legs his major denunciation, often repeated, concerned shared men's and women's toilet facilities in French cafés. Eventually I pointed out to him that this was equally the case on British corridor trains, whether or not they were taking passengers to or from France. He replied that this was irrelevant, and appealed to my mother for support, but this was declined on the grounds that it was an indelicate subject. My father hurriedly walked out, uncharacteristically speechless. The only other time I ever saw him similarly lost for words was when I questioned him about the Thirty-nine Articles of the Church of England, into which I had been dipping at the back of my prayer book during a dull sermon.

Hardham's was among the few local shops that had a sign over its door saying 'You May Telephone from Here'. Telephones were still few and far between in shops and even rarer in private houses, and were considered essential only for professional offices. There were not yet public call boxes on the streets or at the local railway stations. I overheard my Uncle Joe telling a neighbour that Hardham's probably needed their phone to support an under-the-counter sideline of taking bets, which were then allowed to be placed only at racecourses or by mail or telephone to a bookmaker.

The lady florist, whose shop was next door, also cultivated a lengthy strip of garden alongside the rail track close to Woodside station, and was said to have served in the Women's Land Army during the war. She wore men's breeches, and had the reputation of being the rudest shopkeeper for miles around, until her manner changed for the better and she took to wearing skirts. Opinions at home and among our neighbours were divided as to which was the cause, and which the effect, of this transformation.

*

Soon after I was first taken to the High Street, a branch of Sainsbury's opened there. In those days, long prior to its super-market involvement, Sainsbury's sold only 'perishables', with a strong emphasis on meat, poultry and provisions, and no groceries or packaged foods. For some reason that has always puzzled me, the meat section of their stores sold only mutton, lamb and pork, but not beef. Visits to the High Street branch always appealed to me for the framed prints of fancy poultry on its walls. My Uncle Joe told me that they were the work of Ludlow, the great Victorian portrayer of domestic livestock. Later on I collected and treasured some of these prints when they were included in issues of *Feathered World*, which became my favourite weekly, as I disdained children's comics almost as soon as I could read.

The High Street fishmonger was a Greek whose name was Balumi, who came from Salonika. To the conventionally accepted range available in the other fish shops he added fresh salmon, pilchards and sardines, then normally sold only tinned. He was an enthusiastic salesman and persistently extolled the tastiness of local freshwater fish such as carp, perch and pike, but apparently with little effect on the conservative habits of his customers.

Later, when I was at school in Croydon, I got to know his son, who was about my age. He showed me how to catch crayfish in the shallow pools of an abandoned gravel pit. He dropped in fish heads for bait and then doused them with an aniseed cordial. When the crayfish gathered to feed they were easily but cautiously picked off, wrapped in water weed and consigned to a sack. His father paid him twopence each for his catch, to be sold in the shop. I took some home for my mother to cook, but she rejected them as 'vermin'.

In adult life, my neighbours in rural Provence, where crayfish are highly esteemed, employed a similar strategy with a sheep's head and a bottle of pastis. Half the contents of the bottle enveloped the bait, the other half serving to sustain the patience of the fisher. As pastis becomes cloudy on contact with water, the hands needed the protection of stout gloves while groping for the catch.

During the middle years of my childhood – I think about 1925 – a branch of Woolworth's appeared in the High Street. In those days everything they sold was priced at either threepence or sixpence, and the range of choice was amazingly vast, indeed even wider than it became after the abandonment of the limitation. In some few instances it was craftily sidestepped, as for example, by pairs of 'gem-set' cufflinks priced each one of the pair separately.

Woolworth's were then far ahead of Marks & Spencers, whose stores seemed dowdy and unenterprising in choice of merchandise, despite a much higher price limit of three shillings.

At the larger Woolworth branch in central Croydon, I saw and heard for the first time a speak-your-weight slot machine. These became very popular for a time, and their disappearance after only a year or so seems surprising. My mother disapproved of them vehemently, claiming that it was an infringement of her privacy for her weight to be announced to 'all and sundry' who might be within earshot. Perhaps she was expressing a prevailing public disquiet which brought about their demise.

*

The High Street ended at the clock tower, a miniature version of Westminster's Big Ben. Its counterpart I later discovered at the centre of Victoria, the capital of the Seychelles in the Indian Ocean, where I resided for several years. Continuing beyond the clock tower, the uninteresting Selhurst Road, served by elderly and noisy trams, eventually reached West Croydon station. The Croydon tram network was municipally owned and was said to incur heavy operating losses, that were greatly increased whenever track needed re-laying due to road resurfacing. The trams were long overdue for replacement, and while I was still at school a fleet of trolley buses took over from them.

Facing the clock tower was the South Norwood Police Station, where my father sometimes called in to see old friends from his wartime service with the Special Constabulary. His regular duty on the night watch had been to guard a lonely foot-path subway under the railway against sabotage by enemy agents. Armed only with a truncheon, a police whistle and a bicycle lamp, it seems improbable that he would have been able to foil a prepared and determined assault. When I was with him I might be taken to see the horses stabled at the rear if they were not on patrol, as they usually were on a Saturday if there was a game at the nearby Crystal Palace football ground. Every big match played there was preceded by the spectators singing the hymn 'Abide With Me', led by a conductor. Why this particular hymn alone, and no other, I wondered? Whatever the custom's origin, it has endured to be still lingering on at the century's end. Although I was never interested in the game I felt a natural allegiance to the Palace club, then far down in the league, which greatly amused my Uncle Joe, who supported Millwall, then at the top of it.

To the left of the clock tower was Station Road, the short approach to Norwood Junction. It was said that before it became a junction, with a branch line to the Crystal Palace, the station was called Jolly Sailor, and a public house of this name, from which it was borrowed, still existed in the High Street.

On one corner of Station Road was a paint shop on which the rainbow-hued fascia announced its owner as Euan Tudball, Colourman. When I was reading the Sherlock Holmes stories later on, I imagined that he had drawn this description of his trade from 'The Adventure of the Retired Colourman', until I learnt that it was because he had been a colour sergeant in the Army. When my Grandfather Silverwood came to stay with us he used to take me in with him to see Mr Tudball, a fellow enthusiast with whom he engaged in animated discussions about pigments, linseed oils and varnishes. To alleviate his defective hearing, Mr Tudball carried an ivory ear trumpet, hanging from a cord around his neck when not in use. Deafness was much more prevalent then than later on, or probably it was more evident before the introduction of electronic hearing aids. Elderly folk were commonly presumed to be more or less deaf, and were spoken to loudly and slowly, which must have been irritating to those whose hearing was not in fact impaired.

On the opposite corner was an architectural ironmongery stocked with elaborate fittings that were presumably in demand for the large houses on South Norwood Hill. It was run by a Mrs Halestrap, a widow who was renowned as a locksmith. On one occasion when I was taken there by my Grandmother Hutchings for a key to be cut, Mrs Halestrap lifted me on to a tall safe and asked me what was the first thing I would do if I wanted to open it and I had no key? I guessed at the lockpick, then at a charge of explosive, but both answers were wrong. 'The first thing is to check whether it's locked,' she said. 'That's something useful to be remembered all your life – not because it's a safe, but because the answer applies to many other problems you'll encounter in everyday life.'

Along one side leading to the station most of the premises were occupied by solicitors and accountants. There was also an estate agent called Burcote, claiming to be 'also at Sackville Street, Piccadilly, London W1'. Its particulars of properties for sale were displayed in the window on cards mounted on miniature easels. This was then the only estate agency in the district, as in those days almost all the houses, other than the large ones on South Norwood Hill, were rented.

Next door was the Registry of Births, Deaths and Marriages. Standing at the kerb outside there was usually a grim-faced, shabbily dressed man bearing a large board scrawled with a lengthy message that had weathered to become almost unreadable. He was said to be protesting at the lack or loss of his birth registration. My father once advised him to apply to the Central Registry at Somerset House in London. 'I've spent years campaigning there too, but they ignore me,' he replied. 'You see, they're a party to the conspiracy!'

When I first knew Station Road a large building on the other side was the headquarters of Payne & Birdseye, haulage contractors with horse-drawn vehicles, but it was later demolished to be replaced by a cinema. Although modest in comparison with

49

many built during the postwar years, it was such an improvement on the old Portland Road cinemas that we were encouraged to hope that my mother could be persuaded to give it a trial. For as long as I could remember she had refused to set foot in one because, she insisted, it would give her a headache, or in her own words, 'bring on one of my heads'. As it turned out, the new one transformed her attitude. A severe thunderstorm during a shopping expedition with Aunt May drove them to shelter in its vestibule. When my mother complained of feeling faint, the doorman escorted them to seats just inside the auditorium. The film in progress was an instalment of the then-popular serial 'The Perils of Pauline'. My mother's faintness recovered and she became so engrossed that she returned to see the next episode, and thereafter was a confirmed cinemagoer.

The nearest big cinemas were in central Croydon, where the Davis opened when I was at school nearby. It was then reputed to be the largest in Europe, and was among the first to have a café, a Wurlitzer organ mounted on an ascending podium, and to stage variety acts between films. The New Victoria at London's Elephant and Castle challenged its claim to size, but for both of them a vast auditorium provided serious acoustic problems when sound films were introduced in 1927.

*

At the side of the station building was the entrance to the goods yard, and here was the office of our coal merchants, Moger & Company. When we went there to place an order it was recorded in a great leather-bound ledger, and again when the account was settled. On the counter were samples in small black dishes that I was told were carved from coal. I can recall only Derby Brights, Tyne Main and Tilmanstone Nuggets – the latter from the Kent coalfield, as my mother told me proudly.

Inside the goods yard there was an enclosed parking area for coster barrows, which were let out to the street-market traders and to itinerant rag-and-bone and scrap-metal collectors. I wondered for a time why those who used them always pushed from the front end rather than from the back, where there were handles, until my father explained that the barrows were originally intended to be donkey-drawn, the handles being cut-down vestiges of the shafts. Consequently, to push from the rear would involve lifting the handles and the weight of the load, whereas from the front it required only downward pressure. I never saw a donkey-drawn barrow locally, although they were still a familiar sight along the Mile End Road when we visited our relatives in the East End. Wagons drawn by mule teams were also to be seen there plying to and from the London Docks, but I never saw them elsewhere. An exotic sight locally were period-style 'way out West' covered wagons drawn by oxen, that I used to see occasionally delivering to Liptons and some other retailers in the High Street. Wagon and team were represented on packets of Atora beef suet as its trade mark, and my mother refused to believe me that I ever encountered them in reality.

In a kiosk on the station forecourt a jobbing printer plied his craft with a small treadle-operated press. My mother took me there once to order labels for her apple jelly, for which the recipe came from my godfather's housekeeper. She took pride in presenting it to friends and neighbours in glass jam jars, of which the supply was limited as most were then of stoneware. The greatly admired rosy colour of the jelly was due less to the fruit than to the addition of cochineal powder. She was briefly disconcerted when my Uncle Wally commented that this was prepared from ground insects, but recovered her composure when reminded that he was a confirmed legpuller.

The Norwood Junction platforms were provided with slot machines, as were most railway stations at that time. There were scent machines that offered tiny phials of Californian Poppy, Jockey Club or Ashes of Roses. Chocolate vending machines offered penny bars of Cadbury's milk and Rowntree's plain, or thicker bars of Fry's nut-milk for twopence. On the downline platform from London there was also a machine vending a Scottish nougat bar called My Queen. My Grandfather Silverwood always brought me one of these when he came to see us. I disliked it because it was sweet and sticky, but I didn't like to tell him so.

The only other confectionery product I ever came across in a vending machine was the Swiss chocolate Toblerone in its characteristic triangular section bars. The sole machine was oddly sited in a country lane on the Isle of Wight against a hedgerow bounding a meadow, distant from houses or shops and from the nearest crossroads or turning. Why there, I wondered? Many years later, as an adult, I encountered a Toblerone marketing executive and mentioned my curiosity to him. He was equally puzzled and took the trouble to phone his head office in Switzerland. The archivist in charge of its house museum there could find no record that the product had ever been available in vending machines, anywhere.

Weighing machines were sited on almost every station platform, and there was also one chained to the wall outside our local chemist shop. My mother distrusted it and instead took me into the shop to be weighed non-mechanically, which involved a calibrated scale with a sliding balance to be adjusted by hand.

Also at Norwood Junction, and at some other stations at which travellers might need to wait for a connection, there was a slot machine for embossing nameplates on metal strips. A dial had letters and figures around its rim, a centrally pivoted pointer to select them, and a lever to activate the embossing punch. A penny provided 25 punches, and another would be required if the text needed any more. To complete the operation, another lever delivered the finished product, rounded neatly at each end, with holes provided to affix it. I punched my name on this machine on several occasions, but never found a use for the results. Another occasional platform slot machine provided pennyworths of electric shocks: 'Safe, invigorating electrotherapy for all ages – insert coin'.

It was on the Norwood Junction platforms that I first noticed the porters wearing waistcoats with attached sleeves, but no jackets, which was the general practice on the railways, although unknown otherwise. Waistcoats were essential components of the three-piece suit, and style-conscious wearers left the lowest button undone, a custom said to have been established by the Prince of Wales. The tailoring trade tried to popularise double-breasted waistcoats after the war, but with little success, as their wear soon became associated with 'bounders', as did the early introduction of suede shoes. Bounders were individuals who transgressed the accepted code of their class, however harmlessly, whereas cads were those guilty of positively antisocial behaviour. This censorious use of the word 'cad' was relatively recent, as earlier in the century it was the vernacular term for a bus conductor, and both my grandfathers still used it in that sense.

*   *   *

My Hutchings grandparents came to stay with us for a while when they were househunting. They had decided to uproot from the East End when grandfather retired and to live in our district, 'but essentially within sight of the Crystal Palace,' he insisted. He was a devotee of the Palace, and was proud to have been born in 1851, the year it was constructed for the Great Exhibition in Hyde Park.

On most fine afternoons during their stay I went out with my grandmother as she searched for a suitable dwelling. On the first of these expeditions she hesitated as we left the house, so I boldly set off to the right instead of in my mother's habitual direction to Portland Road. For a few paces I feared a recall, but then we were safely on our way to the unexplored and hitherto forbidden Albert Road.

My initial impression as we turned the corner was that it was more like a country lane than a suburban thoroughfare. Bounded by trees on each side, the road was downhill into the middle distance and then rose steeply to be lost from sight in the wooded heights of Upper Norwood, crowned by the Crystal Palace.

Opposite the end of our road there was an extensive area of farmland, that later in the century was saved from development to become a nature reserve. Along its boundary was a bridleway and footpath leading to the Elmer's End neighbourhood of Beckenham. Nobody I asked could tell me who Elmer had been, or how he came to his end there.

Beyond the farm were some ancient flint-walled cottages and then a few shops. The first of them was the corn chandler's to which my invited visit with Wally Millward had been denied. This was meagrely stocked and compared unfavourably with Sanders Brothers in Portland Road.

Albert Road's only grocery never failed to arouse my curiosity. It was in a perpetual state of chaos, with unpacked crates and hampers littering the floor and the windows piled with discarded cartons. Despite this uninviting disarray, the business survived, with no evidence of any effort to reform to tidier habits.

54

My grandmother described it as a 'rogue shop'. I have since come across others of the same kind elsewhere, and they all had an undeniably wilful appeal. For several years after the Second World War, a rogue pharmacy survived in London's Soho, its eccentric owner becoming increasingly dishevelled and unkempt. When I asked once for aspirin tablets there he looked bewildered, saying, 'I suppose I must have them somewhere, but I've no idea where I could have put them.' Perhaps his business survived on illicit transactions, since he appeared to attract little legitimate trade.

A Chinese laundry with exotic characters painted on its fascia was the only one in the district, and indeed one of the only two that I have ever encountered in England, the other in the Midlands town of Walsall. Odd this, considering the enduring currency of the phrase 'like a Chinese laundry ticket', to refer to an indecipherable written message.

There was only one public house in the road, an imposing corner building named The Albert Tavern. It was bombed during the Second World War and was later demolished and replaced by a less distinguished structure which claimed to support two cricket teams of which the members and their supporters congregated in separate bars. Whenever we passed the Tavern, the same anxious-looking, raggedly dressed man was standing on the corner opposite the entrance. 'Doubtless he's waiting for anyone he knows who can be persuaded to invite him inside,' said my grandmother. She added that he, and many others like him, were probably widowers living on sufferance in the homes of married daughters or daughters-in-law, and were turned out of the house every day after breakfast to get them 'from under my feet' and 'out of the way'.

Further on were the byres and yard of Sait's dairy, with grazing meadows for the cows beyond. Hens providing the shop's eggs foraged in the yard, still the prewar favourite breeds, Black Minorcas and Buff Orpingtons, soon to be displaced in popularity by White Leghorns and Rhode Island Reds. The advent of nondescript-looking hybrid strains was far into the future, when most hens would be banished from farmyards and confined in batteries.

At the foot of the hill a turning on the left led to the upper end of Portland Road, and this was the way my grandmother took to return home by bus. An Anglican church there would have been the nearest alternative for my parents after my father's dismissal from the parish church, but its proximity to Albert Road was unacceptable to my mother.

Opposite the church was a branch public library which I later frequented as a schoolboy. One day I was held in conversation in the reading room by a man who said he was an out-of-work engineer and the victim of a conspiracy. He claimed to have discovered or invented a new or previously unrecognised mechanical movement, but had been prevented from exploiting it and driven to destitution by the orthodox engineering 'establishment'. After giving vent to his diatribe, which I guessed that he delivered to any easy listener, he proved usefully knowledgeable about local history. He told me that lavender had formerly been grown on the fields along Albert Road and elsewhere in the district, to supply the perfume mills at Mitcham, on the other side of Croydon, where many acres of it were still cultivated. Many years later, when I was living in the lavender-growing area of Provence, I found that a favoured variety there was called Mitcham, but its farmers were unaware that it was named after the place where it originated. While I lived in Woodside, lavender was still being hawked in the streets by groups of Gypsy women chanting their tuneful cry, "Won't you buy my blooming lavender?', that I believe went back to mediaeval times. It was soon to become just a fragrant memory here, but some 50 years later I was surprised and delighted to hear the same cry called again, the same tune but to French words, in the streets of Paris.

*

The young man in charge of the branch library told my grand-mother and me that the remnants of woodland and the ancient trees along Albert Road were the surviving traces of the Great North Wood that once enveloped all Norwood from beyond the Crystal Palace site. The Wood was formerly a favoured haunt of the Gypsies, he said, and that some of their Queens were buried at Gypsy Hill, close the Palace site. Queen Margaret Finch, who died in 1740, was buried in a cubical coffin. She is reputed to have passed her later years in a favoured position, crouched on the ground with her knees drawn up to her chin, and her mourners were unable to straighten out her corpse. He also told us that the road was a section of the old trading route from the Kentish farmlands, and that during the first half of the nine-teenth century a stagecoach plied along it between Chatham and Rochester and the City of London.

Albert Road bore much less traffic than Portland Road and was free of bus routes, and so it was favoured by drivers of horse-drawn vehicles. The carriageway was still paved with granite cobbles, providing a sure footing for the horses, whose iron-shod hooves produced occasional sparks on impact. The most imposing horses – Shires or Clydesdales – drew the brewery drays. They were groomed and harnessed in showground style, and their vehicles were maintained in proud company livery. There were three local breweries, and the London brewer Whitbread also delivered in the area. The latter's horses, still functioning at the century's end, are those used to draw the Lord Mayor's coach in the annual City of London procession.

Brewery dray horses were usually bay or grey, but coal mer-chants preferred black shires with white 'feathered hocks'. Their wagons were either back-loading with a rising prow, or sideloading with a central divide. The company name, borne on the prow or the divide, would be prominently lettered on a ground of a chosen colour. Our regular merchant, Moger, employed a black ground, which I thought uninteresting, but some others used shades of red: Cockerell and Rickett Smith (later amalgamated) were in scarlet, but the brightest was Jno. Pegg of Penge, whose wagons were resplendent in vermilion.

The spectacularly tall all-black funeral horses of Feldwicks, the undertakers in Portland Road, were stabled in a mews off Albert Road. These horses came from Holland, where they continued in use long after their special function became almost entirely motorised in Britain. It was said that a Dutch horse dealer named Cryspeerdt, who had livery stables in Upper Norwood, was the first to introduce them to Britain.

For the most elaborately staged funerals the team of horses drawing the hearse were draped in black velvet and wore black ostrich plumes on their heads. Funerals of this status would be attended by professional mourners, known as 'mutes', who walked alongside the coffin as it was borne to and from the hearse, holding black-edged handkerchiefs to their eyes. The coffin, viewed through the glass panels of the hearse, was closed on a white paper liner, of which the pleated edges were left projecting outside. These liners were prepared by specialists called funeral crimpers, one of whom lived and worked opposite my Silverwood grandparents. He was the father of the actor Jack Warner, who played the policeman Dixon of Dock Green in the classic television series, and of Elsie and Doris Waters, the cockney radio comediennes, who were at school with my mother. When not performing, the sisters' voices were punctiliously ladylike. Authentic cockney speech was still prevalent in the East End, at least in the non-Jewish areas. Later on, after the Second World War, a refined, gentrified version of cockney spread widely throughout Greater London, to become known as 'estuarine' English.

*

The cabs serving Norwood Junction and the central Croydon railway stations were still mostly horse-drawn – four-wheel 'growlers' or hansoms – until well into the 1920s before motor vehicles replaced them.

Household refuse was collected by horse-drawn wagons. The bins were emptied into large baskets by the dustmen, to be tipped into the uncovered and stinking dustcart. The dustmen wore slouch hats with the wide brim turned up on one side and tethered to the crown. Another council vehicle often seen during summer was the water tanker spraying the roads, replenishing its load at local hydrants.

The horses used by the milkmen and other house-calling tradesmen were lighter and finer in build than the heavyweight draught animals, and were known as 'vanners'. They were trained to vary their pace, walking or trotting, and if making repeated calls they would respond to a shout or whistle from their driver as he left each house, and move forward to the next stop. They also remembered at which front gate to expect a regular titbit of a piece of apple or a sugar lump. Another intelligent trained horse seen frequently in our road drew the Carter Paterson parcel van. This service operated countrywide with a network of depots, and provided speedy collection and delivery between household addresses. Local van men patrolled the streets to stop when hailed or when they saw the CP card displayed in a window. The company was absorbed into the nationalised British Road Services soon after the Second World War and its ubiquitous efficiency has never been equalled since.

'Vanner' horses were generally uninteresting in appearance and colour, except the piebalds favoured by the itinerant scrap-metal collectors. The only other piebald I ever saw – apart from at the circus – drew a dilapidated van that had once been an ambulance and was driven by two nuns of the Order of Poor Clares. They collected food waste tipped indiscriminately into rusty metal bins. I thought how very poor they must be to live on such a repulsive diet until my grandmother explained that they collected to feed their pigs, not themselves.

Chestnut-colour horses were rumoured to be of uncertain temper, if not positively vicious. This was certainly true of one that drew a vegetable hawker's cart that plied weekly in our road. This trader aroused my curiosity, because we also saw him street hawking when we went to visit family friends in Barnet, as far north as we were south in London's outer suburbs. What could the connection be? Surely he could have found less inconveniently separated beats?

A similarly puzzling question arose during a holiday on the Kent coast, where a haberdashery shop in a small village announced over its doorway that it was 'Also at Sunbury-on-Thames'. And how could it have come about that an off-licence shop in Portland Road was tied to Lacon's brewery at Great Yarmouth? There must have been countless other outlets in Greater London that would have been much more convenient for stock deliveries, but this was the only one I ever came across in later years. In addition to Lacon's bottled beers this shop also supplied Hammerton's Oatmeal Stout, a long-forgotten beverage brewed in Brixton, South London, and a favourite of some of our neighbours, both men and women.

My parents were total abstainers from their schooldays, when they had 'signed the pledge', but they deviated later in life, I think from when I brought them samples of my home-grown wine from Provence. During my childhood, our next-door neighbour Len Norris made repeatedly thwarted efforts to persuade my father to imbibe Scotch whisky at their Christmas parties. Defeat was eventually conceded one year, and a bottle of ginger wine was placed at his elbow with assurances that it was non-alcoholic, 'like ginger beer'. My father consumed most of it during the early part of the evening, and then slept soundly in his chair until after the usual sit-down supper was over and cleared away. Next morning he remarked to my mother how odd it was that the Norrises hadn't served a Christmas evening meal that year.

All through my childhood Christmas Day was spent at the Silverwood grandparents' home. Great Uncle Joe, grandfather's elder brother, would come up from Ashford in Kent with the home-reared turkey which, after trussing and stuffing and preparation of the giblets, was taken to the local baker's shop to be roasted, along with many others, in the bread oven. Oddly, as it now seems looking back, the sage and onion stuffing was not freshly made but was prepared from a packaged mixture made by Pannet & Needen under their Peahen trademark, and the only 'dry goods' product I ever saw offered by greengrocery shops then.

*   *   *

The long fine summer of 1922 seemed to go on without end in sight, until my euphoria was brought to a shattering standstill by my first day at school. I was totally unprepared: I had no prior experience of other children in groups or crowds, and there was nobody of my age to tell me about this puzzling new environment. My parents evidently thought that 'now it's time for school' explained itself and everything I would need to understand.

The first I knew about starting school that day was when my father roused me early for breakfast and told me that on his way to the station he would be taking me to Miss Balfour's Lister House, the local 'dame school'. He insisted that I had porridge with my breakfast, although it always made me feel sick. He never ate it himself, as he claimed it disagreed with him.

A crowd of children was already gathering noisily outside Lister House as we went to the front door – the only time I ever entered by it. We were admitted by a lady I came to know as Young Miss Smith, one of the teachers, and led upstairs to Miss Balfour's study, an untidy room about which my father commented with disapproval to my mother that evening. Miss Balfour was also untidy, and ever afterwards I associated her with a heavy waft of lavender water. Asleep on her desk was a ginger cat, an unusual colour locally at that time, and I later discovered that it had another unusual characteristic of an extra toe on each foot.

After introducing me, my father was instructed to leave me with the others outside to wait for the school bell, a card with my surname and initial was pinned to my jacket, and we departed.

My sense of desolation as my father left me outside was abysmal. The nearest children on the edge of the throng fell silent and stared at me with hostile expressions. Then a boy larger than me grabbed the cap from my head and demanded 'What's this, then?' This was an expensive tweed head-dress in authentic adult style, made-to-measure by an immigrant hatter in Whitechapel with the appropriate name of Topperman. Pointless to explain this. 'We wear proper caps here, with the school badge on them,' continued my inquisitor. 'Not rubbish like this,' he added, flinging my cap over the front garden hedge, where I deemed it wise to abandon it, for the time being, at least.

I did my best to make myself inconspicuous as the jeering laughter at my discomfiture subsided, until a small girl sidled up to me and asked what the initial on my name card stood for. Uncertain how to respond, I stayed silent. 'Come on, I like you,' she said. 'You can tell me in secret, and I promise not to tell anyone else.' So I whispered it, and to my dismay she immediately shouted it out and aroused further hoots of laughter. I was so appalled by this wicked breach of confidence that I would not have been surprised had a thunderbolt descended to strike her down for her treachery. The experience of a few minutes, however, served to fore-arm me against much to come that was previously unimaginable.

*

Formal proceedings began with assembly in the main school-room, a corrugated-iron extension at the rear that became distractingly cold during the winter. Miss Balfour presided from a high desk at the centre of the platform, with the teachers in line behind her. She delivered a short address, to which scant attention was accorded, welcoming new pupils and outlining the school rules. This was followed by a hymn, on this occasion 'All Things Bright and Beautiful'. As it concluded, there was a loud thunderclap. 'Stay calm, children,' she ordered. 'In case anyone feels frightened, I'll read to you from *What Katy Did* before we disperse to our classes.' The teachers left the platform, and the room. Evidently they were not frightened, I thought, or perhaps they had heard Katy often enough already.

*

My experience waiting for the school bell on my first day at Lister House was representative of the way I was to be treated later that day, and subsequently all through the term. The boy who had snatched my cap continued to harass me with varied torments, skilfully applied. Other boys followed his example, except for the few of us who were the perpetual victims, and I seemed to be lowest in the pecking order that term. The girls sometimes made a show of sympathy for me, shallow and often false cover for conspiracies of misinformation to disconcert me and feed added stress to my insecurity.

The teaching was pathetically inadequate, and most of it during that first term I had already learnt at home. The introduction to handwriting was by crayon and slate, copying meaningless arabesques called 'pothooks and hangers' intended to simulate the strokes of copperplate script, but when the time came we were taught what was known as 'Civil Service hand', a simplified upright form. When we proceeded to spelling lessons, they involved a long-outdated word book in which a large proportion of the entries were rare in common usage or obsolete: the first words under initial A, for instance, were Adze, Ague, Alb, Apse, Aspen. A period every morning was devoted to recitation of the multiplication tables, from 'twice two' to 'twelve times twelve'. My father insisted that I also learnt the thirteen times table, which he assured me would prove invaluable, although I cannot recall ever making use of it in later life.

Miss Balfour wandered from class to class absent-mindedly, leaving a lavender-scented trail behind her. Her younger sister, Mrs Braithwaite, played the piano at the morning assembly and for Swedish drill in the afternoon interval. She wore bobbed hair and flapper-fashion clothes and was reputed to have been a chorus girl in Paris at the Moulin Rouge.

Miss Smith taught the second term pupils, and her sister, Young Miss Smith, had charge of the little ones. The older boys and girls were in separate classes. Boys were taught by Mr Braun, an elderly misfit with blotchy complexion and bloodshot eyes, whose perpetually short temper reflected an inherent dislike of children. The older girls' mistress, Mrs Hanhart, wore her grey hair in a tight bun and had a loud and toneless voice that penetrated throughout the school.

At mid-morning there was a break, and watered hot milk was served in battered enamel mugs. I was given a daily penny to spend on my way to school on something to eat during the break. For this I could buy a rock bun at the Cokelers' bakery, or two from the previous day if any were left over, or a small packet of Sun Maid raisins, or a miniature tin of Huntley & Palmer's alphabet biscuits. The latter was my favourite, because the tin – a precise copy of the full-size ones at the grocery – would be treasured long after the tiny biscuits had been eaten, but I soon had to abandon this choice as it was invariably snatched and purloined. Instead, I took to liquorice, which I disliked, of which I could get 16 strings (known as 'bootlaces') at four for a farthing, and which I could distribute to bribe my way to some brief respite from torments.

School dinners typically comprised shepherd's pie or fish cakes with carrots or turnips and sodden cabbage, followed by pudding that resembled stale fruitcake drowned in watery custard. The meals were only cursorily supervised, often by Young Miss Smith, whose authority over the older and more obstreperous boys was minimal.

I dreaded the daily mealtime, and even more the following hour euphemistically called 'playtime'. Everyone seemed to have friends except me, and nobody needed one more. The only apparent prospect was Andrew Parry, a quiet boy who seemed to eschew the noisier and more violent activities, so I asked him, 'Will you be my friend?' He looked me up and down and then beyond me before replying, 'No, I've got one already!' and turned away.

Evidently, this was not the way to go about it, so I thought again. It struck me that the boys who had elder brothers at the school seemed to be less prone to persecution. One of several pairs of brothers were the Greenstreets, Edgar and Bernie, with a good two years separating them, but they were usually close together. They were always the first to instigate new activities, whether seasonal like 'conkers', and wearing favours for the University Boat Race or passing phases such as home-made kites or marbles, played with a large glass jack known as the 'ally tor'. They were skilled at popularising new fashions. One such that term was a pocket comb and mirror for each boy, hitherto restricted to the girls, and it is evidence of the Greenstreet leadership talents that they won over the boys to the idea without difficulty. My own comb and mirror, and those of many others, were confiscated by Mr Braun, in order, he said, to discourage our vanity.

I stayed close to Bernie for the rest of the term, and Edgar was never far away. Sure enough, the proximity proved effective and daily strife became less prevalent, except for one brief, harrowing gap while Edgar was away from school, having his tonsils removed.

The Greenstreet brothers' outstanding success that term was the promotion of the bus ticket 'sevens' collecting craze. This was based on the belief that if one amassed a thousand used tickets bearing numbers terminating in the digit 7, a valuable prize would be won. The nature of the prize and the identity of the authority from which it would be claimed remained obscure. Where to submit a full pack of sevens would have been a problem, as at that time there were many bus operators who plied locally, and throughout greater London. The established companies were London General and Tillings, working together in close collaboration, but there were also the 'pirate' companies competing with them, often with tactics that were condemned as underhand or detrimental to public safety. They would speed past General or Tillings vehicles to grab passengers at a popular pick-up, or vary their routes to increase custom at different times of day or days of the week. They were much favoured by children in lieu of the dull reliability of the 'establishment' services. My own favourites on our local routes were Edward Paul (chocolate livery), Timpson (silver) and Royal Sovereign (crimson).

All the bus services terminated not far beyond Woodside, and country buses and Green Line coaches were far into the future. There were some charabanc excursions to country beauty spots and the seaside during spring and summer, and evening trips to the London theatres were started, although I believe that they had pre-existed before the war.

*   *   *

Wednesday afternoon was a half-holiday at Lister House, and whenever my mother felt well enough she would collect me at the school gate to visit her family in the East End, where my father would join us from his office. I always enjoyed visits to my Silverwood grandparents and Aunt Rene, but this journey there involved a hazard that added another element of stress to my term-time woes.

To save time and catch the earliest possible train we approached Norwood Junction station by its rear entrance, a narrow and poorly lighted subway, dank and neglected, and a favoured haunt of beggars. I dreaded the prospect of close encounters with them in that confined space, and it became the focus of recurrent nightmares.

From a very early age I was obsessed by a morbid fear of beggars. I guess that this may well have been engendered by one of my father's often-repeated sayings: when complaining about the level of taxation, he would always conclude 'and at this rate they'll have us all begging in the streets!'

At this period, during the early 1920s, many professional beggars reflected the bygone Victorian era and could have stepped out of the pages of Mayhew's books on London's underworld. They bore no resemblance to latter-day mendicants, whose plight, whether real or simulated, is generally projected as temporary misfortune. They plumbed the depths of pity for the pathetically irreversible plight of their afflictions. Their infirmities, deformities or mutilations were histrionically displayed, and often they called out or gestured to draw attention to them. Their questing gaze on passers-by was unfaltering until they caught a sympathetic or unwary eye, when the set facial expression of hopeless misery would be enhanced by a directly targeted servile, fawning appeal. The performance often seemed to me to involve an element of self mockery, as if to imply that 'You and I are both aware that it's over-played, but we'll both feel better if you spare a coin, won't we?'

A legless man, supported on a board fitted with castors, was among my most dreaded encounters, because his eyes were on a level with mine and he seemed to be appealing to me alone of all the passers-by. Another frightening sight was a man who propelled himself along on a wheeled walking frame, violently shaking and shuddering and calling out in a piteously quavering voice. Sightless beggars I feared less than the others, until I realised that there could be imposters among them. This was when one, threatened by a snarling dog, raised his blacked-out spectacles for an instant to reveal a momentary focused glance towards the miscreant.

Yes, this was then in a London suburb, not far away in places like Calcutta or Bombay! My horror at these dreaded sights was coupled with a fascinated curiosity about them. Where did they go when they were 'off-stage'? Later on, I heard it suggested that many of them lived with poor relatives who sent them out to beg so that they could contribute to the family purse, however meagrely. How did they get to and from their pitches? At a time when suburban railway carriages lacked corridors, I shuddered at the possibility that one of them might embark at the next stop, and I feared being taken into a public toilet in case there might be any of them there.

*

The Vagrancy Act and local by-laws prohibited soliciting for alms in public, but were virtually unenforced. Many mendicants sought to evade possible indictment by offering something for sale, usually a token box of matches or a pair of bootlaces, or by musical performance, vocal or instrumental. Few street singers showed any evidence of ability, except for the choirs of unemployed Welsh miners. Instrumental offerings were somewhat more variable in quality, but rarely rose above the deplorably inadequate.

The entirely unskilled street musicians were the organ grinders. The least degraded of these played piano-simulating barrel organs, popularly known as 'tinglearys'. These were wheeled and hand-pushed, or occasionally drawn by a donkey. It was said that throughout the Greater London area they were owned and rented out by the day by the Pasquale family in Clerkenwell. They seemed to be well maintained, and often played familiar operatic and music-hall tunes.

Smaller instruments, miscalled hurdy-gurdys but properly harmonican organs, with simulated wind effect, were borne on small barrows or old prams. The smallest ones could be mounted on a stick and supported by a belt round the opera-tor's shoulders if he was able to stand upright. These organs were mostly decrepit and usually played dismal hymn tunes. They, and their attendants, were my ultimate horror and dread. The distant glimpse or sound of one in a crowded shopping street, and in an instant I would be violently shaking and sweat-ing. These sudden attacks greatly concerned and puzzled my parents, as I was totally incapable of explaining what caused them. The origin of the phobia still eludes me. Puzzling, this, considering that the first sighting of one that I recall, at the age of about three, brought no reaction at all. Evidently, some sub-sequent experience, expunged from my memory, was to blame. The only clue is that my worst scenario is of an organ being played while being pushed along the street. This I do not remember ever seeing in reality, but a film sequence viewed in adult life caused me such distress that I was impelled to vacate the cinema seat to endure a severe bout of vomiting.

The neurosis continued to afflict me until it was eventually alleviated by encountering the ornate and superbly conserved street organs of Amsterdam, scaled-down versions of the show-men's fairground instruments constructed by the master crafts-men Gavioli and Marenghi. After the last World War, so I have been told, the cards that activate them were devotedly punched by a judge of the Dutch High Court to enliven the streets with the popular tunes of the day.

In Paris, street organs survived for long after their disappear-ance in London, and at least a dozen examples are still circulat-ing at the end of the century, more than I remember when I first lived there in the mid-1930s. In French they were called *orgues de Barbarie*, which I associated with the Barbary Coast until I learnt that it was a misspelling of Berberi, the eighteenth-century maker who was claimed to have originated them. Elsewhere in European cities they can still be seen and heard here and there, notably in Germany, where many of them originated. One seen on the world's television screens during the demolition of the Berlin Wall was in charge of a grinder incongruously – it seemed to me – wearing a bowler hat.

The traditional association of monkeys with street organs has survived in popular allusions such as 'talking to the organ grinder, not the monkey', but during a lifetime's observation I have seen only a single example. This was in Croydon, in about 1925, and the pathetic little creature was not performing or collecting coins but wrapped in rags in a cardboard box and protected under a glass case. Its eyes were closed in sleep – or was it not alive?

*

Not long after I left Lister House to go to school in Croydon the beggars vanished from our streets, so suddenly and completely that I was puzzled as to how and why, and have been wondering about it ever since. Was it the result of more stringent regulation, local or national? Or effective police action to clear kerbside obstructions to increasing vehicle traffic? Or concerted efforts between local authority and charities? Whatever the answers may be, the question remains: what happened to them: where did they go, and who became responsible for them?

When some beggars were eventually seen again in the streets they were a different breed: cadgers, improvidents and unemployed, but evidently not without hope, and certainly not professional exhibitionists like those I had feared, the leftovers from a previous age.

*   *   *

71

The Wednesday return journey was free of apprehension about the subway, as we always left the station by its front entrance and caught a bus. On one train ride back, another boy from Lister House was in the same compartment as us with his parents.

His name was Jack Winter, although for some reason he was always known as 'Speedy'. He was to become my first school friend – indeed, my first friend – and later, when we left Lister House, we went on to school in Croydon together. We shared a lack of conformity, but whereas I tried to conceal mine, Speedy flaunted his eccentricity and yet seemed to be proof against the attentions of the bullies and taunters. To be 'different' was to be vulnerable, but I guess that a sufficiently marked difference became a protection because the conformists felt out of their depth as to how to react to it. Also, my constant effort to be inconspicuous itself drew attention to my being alien to the majority.

Speedy had a marked tendency to move sideways in crab-like manner, and as he grew older his physical appearance seemed to me to take on a close resemblance to G.K. Chesterton's description of his character Father Brown. He chattered interminably, sometimes irrespective of whether anyone was listening. He was a tireless advocate of enthusiasms, for which he sought converts with evangelical fervour. These causes, which changed frequently, were usually schemes advertised to promise instant success of one kind or another. When I first got to know him, it was a book promoting '101 Secret Formulae'. This claimed to reveal how to produce household products such as cleansers, polishes and solvents at home without special ingredients or equipment. It was followed by 'Be a Stamp Dealer', for which stock and kit was supplied, including a rubber stamp moulded with your chosen business name. This one had been advertised in the schoolboys' weekly, *The Magnet*, which recorded the fictional exploits of Harry Wharton and Billy Bunter of Greyfriars School.

I do not recall that any of his 'get rich quick' schemes brought him anything like the results promised for them. One that ended disastrously involved Indian Runner ducks: 'The Supreme Layers – Fresh Eggs Every Day!' His response to the tempting offer in *Exchange and Mart* brought him a dozen young ducklings to be reared, but no eggs ever eventuated from them. The advertiser claimed that they were sexed before dispatch, and so they were proved to have been: they all turned out to be drakes.

Later, at our big school, Speedy started a junior magazine, of which only one issue appeared before his attention was usurped by another project. My contribution was a short story about buried treasure, his was an Ode to Arcturus, which involved words beyond the normal schoolboy vocabulary such as 'transplendent' and 'etiolated'. Our form master expressed the opinion that if it was to be followed by others of similar erudition it would be wise to append a glossary. Speedy explained that he had composed his poem with the guidance of a free sample lesson received from an advertiser in *John o' London's Weekly*, then the indispensable mentor of literary aspirants. He claimed that it was his ambition to become a professional author, for which he was in the course of deciding on his choice of a *nom de plume.* It was a widely-held conception at that time that the pseudonym was indispensable to authorship.

He and his mother were devoted churchgoers, with an eclectic taste in Anglican services, sampling a different church on most Sundays. During my adolescent Anglo-Catholic phase I made strenuous efforts to gain his adherence to the faith, but with a double-edged effect when he converted to Rome, in sympathy with my arguments.

In senior school I saw him less after our academic paths separated: he became a shining light of the science wing, while I studied classics. He left school the term before me to a post in the analytical department of Shuttleworth's chocolate factory at Mitcham. I last saw him at an Armistice service at the Croydon War Memorial. He was brimming with optimism for the prospects of chocolate-coated ice cream, which he claimed to have invented, but I never heard whether he benefited from its market launch the following year. His flow of enthusiasm was interrupted by the Remembrance silence, and when I turned to him as it concluded, he was already confiding in somebody else. I left him to it, and departed to what seemed at the time to be some more pressing activity.

I never saw him again. It would not have been difficult to keep in touch, but I simply failed to make the effort. I have lost other friends in this remiss way during my lifetime, to my great regret in later years. Someone once wrote that 'Friendship must be cultivated or it withers away.' True enough, as expressed in English, but when I quoted it to a Frenchman he reproved me. I had not yet then appreciated that to a peasant the French verb '*cultiver*' implies 'to cultivate with the object of profit'.

*   *   *

Soon after the end of term my father took me to the Crystal Palace to ascend one of its towers, both of which had been closed to the public until then since the beginning of the war. It was the Lord Mayor's Show day in London, on which, for some arcane reason, his office always closed for the occasion.

The tower lift rose very slowly and creaked a great deal. We were the only passengers, and the attendant plied us with information about the extent of the view to be seen aloft, including, he claimed, no less than four surviving windmills, at Shirley, Wimbledon, Keston and Brixton. Unfortunately, fewer lifts are operated by attendants in later years, as I have always found them to be usefully informative characters, comparable in this respect to taxi drivers and hall porters at large hotels.

The view from the summit observation platform was astonishingly impressive: all London seemed to be spread out beneath our eyes. The lift man left his cabin to join us for a few minutes until called down again, and pointed out Hampstead Heath, Primrose Hill, the Alexandra Palace, and the newly built site of the British Empire Exhibition at Wembley, to which we paid a visit soon after. Regretfully, my recollection of the Exhibition is negligible, except for a descent into a mock-up coal mine, a rowdy amusement park, and a popular tune of the time called 'When it's Night-time in Italy it's Wednesday Over Here'.

On the south side the view across Croydon extended far into Surrey, passing beyond Box Hill, Farthing Down and Crohamhurst Heights to the western slopes of the North Downs.

On the following year's Lord Mayor's Show day my father took me to Crohamhurst for the first time, and it was there that we came across the Magpie Man, of whom I had heard tell in Woodside. He was said to be a disgraced former bank manager 'come down in the world' and now 'living in distressed circumstances'. His claim to attention was a brood of magpies perching on a sack across his shoulders, and one or two of them sometimes on his hat. They were free to fly away, but never strayed far before returning. From time to time he would moisten morsels of bread in his mouth and place them between his lips, to allow the birds to feed from him. He told us that he had rescued them newly hatched when their mother was killed by a predator. Before we left for home he took us to see nests of the gold-crested wren, the pied wagtail and the bullfinch.

On the way back I questioned why we were not calling him 'Magpie Jack'. My father said, 'That wouldn't be appropriate, because he's a gentleman.'

'But Christmas Tree Jack speaks like a gentleman,' I protested.

'Well, he can't be one to be making such a public spectacle of himself,' was the reply.

*   *   *

Shortly before the school holiday ended my grandmother took me with her to view a property that was offered for sale nearby. It was a detached house in a mostly terraced road with a single shop, a grocery that also sold household goods and would in later times be described as a general store. On the pavement outside it stood an octagonal Queen Victoria pillar box. The house we went to see was claimed to have been lived in by Sir Arthur Conan Doyle during his early medical career. Later, when reading the Sherlock Holmes stories, I liked to think that it was the original of the house described in 'The Norwood Builder'.

Further along the road was a derelict house in an advanced state of neglect and dilapidation, one of a number of similar properties locally that were said to have belonged to war victims whose relatives could not be traced. The Norris girls next door to us called them 'ghost houses' and warned me that they were the haunt of tramps. Looking back, I think this was improbable: tramps in those days routinely trudged between Casual Wards, and would disdain to shelter under even less comfortable conditions. Mostly, they seemed to pursue their lifestyle with a sense of independence and innate dignity. My father likened them to medieval friars who took pride in their freedom from the burdens of property and family responsibilities. This was one day when a tramp asked him politely if he could spare a penny to get a cup of tea. My father felt in his pocket, but had no coppers, so he offered the man a sixpence, which was refused, with thanks: 'I only need the penny,' he said. They were a class apart from professional beggars. If they sometimes knocked at a back door during their travels, it would be where they might expect to be offered a bite to eat or discarded garments. Such houses were known to the tramping fraternity, and were usually distinguished by a discreet chalk mark on a garden fence or gatepost.

*   *   *

My second term at Lister House began, and continued, less harrowingly than the first, even though Edgar Greenstreet had left, to work at the garage in Portland Road. The improvement derived largely, I think, from the birthday party my father organised during the holiday at the Congregational church hall, and to which all the pupils of around my age were invited. Everyone agreed that it was an outstanding success. My father drew upon his experience of organising Sunday-school treats, and there is no doubt that he was good with children in numbers, even though less skilled with a single child – his only son.

He had planned a succession of games, team activities and competitions, and boys and girls were quite remarkably well ordered, in contrast to their school behaviour outside class-time. This may have been partly because the older boys were absent, but essentially it was thanks to my father's expertise.

My mother had prepared tea, with sandwiches and a huge birthday cake, blancmanges and jellies. She was enterprising with jellies, and made them in contrasting layers: each layer needed to set before the next was added, and the whole confection needed to be consumed in one meal or the colours began to leach and spoilt the effect. My aunts May, Rene and Beatie helped her to serve. I was guilty of the only discordant note, I must confess: at the start of the meal I called out jocularly, 'Five sandwiches to be eaten before birthday cake!' When it was time for the cake to be served, one guest (whose identity I am ashamed to have forgotten) refused his slice, protesting wearily, 'No, thank you, I've only just managed to eat my five sandwiches.'

The birthday party brought me a number of return invitations to others, but I was allowed to accept only a few of them that my mother decided came from 'suitable addresses'.

*

On the last day of term two new figures joined the line-up of teachers at the morning assembly. Miss Balfour introduced them as Captain and Mrs Cassidy, and announced that they would be taking over the school on her retirement with immediate effect. They were a good-looking and smartly dressed couple, and the older girls, who claimed to be knowledgeable in worldly matters, were confident that the new regime augured promisingly for the future.

My parents, who had been reading about the transfer of ownership in the local newspaper, were impressed that the Cassidys would be a distinguished asset to the school and to the social tone of the neighbourhood. Indeed, the gallant Captain was immediately recruited as a sidesman at the parish church, fulfilling his duty garbed with a graduate's hood, in conformity with the vicar and curate. This was normal in many Anglican churches at which vestments were eschewed as 'Romish', but non-sacramental ritual, such as the elevation of the congregation's offertory before the altar, was elaborated into a dramatic performance.

*   *   *

During my second term at Lister House Grandfather Hutchings had retired, and while I was on holiday my daily outings were usually with him, my grandmother staying at home with my mother, who was in the throes of one of her 'declines'. These occurred from time to time without clearly diagnosed symptoms, and tended to last as long as there was someone to relieve her of her household duties. The family doctor called weekly to upbraid her, which had no evident effect on her condition but doubtless nurtured her self-esteem, as it was customary for the ladies of the neighbourhood to take pride in the outspoken rudeness of their medical practitioners. These were mostly Scots who had qualified before crossing the border, and may have adopted their bedside manner from Glaswegian mentors during their training.

Our doctor vehemently disapproved of my mother's daily consumption of 'beef tea', which monopolised her diet during her periods of decline. 'Enough of these fluids,' I overheard him declaim one day. 'What you need are more solids!' This puzzled me, as the only solids I knew were a set of wooden geometry models reposing on a classroom shelf at school. The term 'solids' also referred to food served on a plate at table, as distinct from a snack taken between meals. My mother insisted that I must always leave something on the plate 'For Miss Manners', which seems an odd parsimony considering that she had recently endured years of wartime food shortages.

*

Even after his retirement Grandfather Hutchings dressed habitually in a dark suit and white shirt with a high starched collar, and blue polka-dot bow tie. For gardening he would don an identical old suit that had been discarded for regular wear, with the starched collar minus the tie – the omission intended, I presume, to indicate that he was not suitably garbed to engage in 'polite company'. As an adult appalled by the way teenagers choose to dress themselves, I wonder what my grandfather thought about my own appearance during that period of my life. An advanced stage of adult horror at teenage fashions is when they are seen being worn by the middle-aged.

*

The first outing with my grandfather involved mounting South Norwood Hill on foot, which I had never been expected to tackle before. The prospect seemed daunting as we crossed the High Street to begin the climb, but he reassured me by saying that we would be paying a call and taking a rest about halfway up.

At the foot of the hill there was a stone horse trough, and beside it waited a trace horse to assist draught vehicles up to the summit. Further on were the Stanley Halls, venues for public functions and amateur entertainment, built and endowed by a local manufacturer of optical instruments, whose factory was alongside Norwood Junction station. Twice a year in the larger of the two halls the Crystal Palace Light Opera Society staged Gilbert and Sullivan performances, to which I was often taken. There were several other amateur light opera companies in the district, but none of them in those days ever presented other than Gilbert and Sullivan. The words and music were still in copyright, and their performance was strictly controlled and monitored by their proprietors, the D'Oyly Carte Company. Every show had to be produced by a licensed professional, in unvarying conformity with a tradition governing every move-ment and gesture and the smallest detail of stage 'business' and knockabout comedy.

*

81

The address we were visiting was named Polygon House. Its occupant was Colonel Saville, retired from the Indian Army with the loss of an arm on a tiger shoot, and a local Councillor. My grandfather's introduction to him had come from the Conservative Party of his former constituency, and subsequently he acted as his election agent as the Ratepayers' candidate. In those days the Conservatives in local government called themselves Ratepayers, to imply that, unlike the Labour Party, they were non-political.

The house owed its name to a many-windowed room with views all round, projecting above the roof. From here, in 1927, I witnessed the total eclipse of the sun with my grandfather and some of the Colonel's other friends. I was intrigued by the haze of violet light that surrounded everything in the half-light as the sun was obscured, but the adults said I imagined it. The next day at school my friend Speedy Winter, and others, confirmed my experience. Could it be that during a solar eclipse the normally visible range of the spectrum is temporarily extended to child eyes?

This was the first of several visits to Polygon House during the school holiday. While the grown-ups discussed their affairs over something poured from a decanter and cheroots, I would enjoy freshly-squeezed lemonade brought by a parlour maid while I looked at books with coloured pictures of wildlife. When I had shown good care of them I was allowed an imposing leather-bound volume on Indian game birds, of which the Colonel was the author, published by the Bombay Natural History Society.

On one fine morning we took a stroll in the grounds, in which some peafowl were kept. Passing out through the gate at the back, we went on to the Norwood Club. In its grounds was a lake, once the headwater of the London to Croydon canal, the reclaimed bed of which became the first railway line to Norwood Junction. My grandfather became a member of the Club, and I spent happy hours there feeding the swans and ducks and watching the fish rise to snatch morsels they overlooked.

82

Outside the gateway to the Club drive was a public convenience, at which my grandfather expressed his indignation at the Council signs MEN and WOMEN, in lieu of GENTLEMEN and LADIES, to which he insisted the ratepayers were entitled. Many years later, during a conversation with him about life in France, I remarked that at least one objective of the French Revolution achieved lasting success: to make every male citizen a gentleman (as in *monsieur*) and every woman a lady (as in *madame*). He agreed that this was a worthy achievement, but reserved his doubts about the merits of the Revolution in other respects.

On our first visit to the Club I noticed Mr Braun from Lister House as we entered the lounge. He rose from his chair to greet Colonel Saville, who nodded curtly and passed on. When we were seated out of earshot, he explained to my grandfather that Mr Braun was a former Conservative Party member who had resigned to join the 'heretical' Social Credit Party. This, he explained, was a political creed originated in Canada by a Major Douglas and brought here with the Canadian forces during the war. When I went on to school in Croydon, I heard more about it from one of the masters who gave lessons on current affairs. It was based on a concept called the 'national dividend'. This meant that whenever new wealth was created, as for instance when coal was brought up from a mine, its value should be distributed into the community to increase purchasing power. The Social Credit Party in this country soon split, the breakaway faction calling itself the National Dividend League. Both bodies held street meetings in Croydon for some time, during which the main activity seems to have been to heckle and create disruption to the opposition.

*

Until Grandfather Hutchings retired he seemed remote in my family life, as whenever I saw him there were always other adults present. With our outings together I had him to myself, and I soon found that we shared interests in subjects I never heard mentioned by my parents.

Minor events or sights could set him off on a trail of reminiscence. On one occasion it was a concertina-playing busker who provided the cue to an account of a music-hall act involving a family of concertina players. The culmination of the performance was a giant instrument requiring a player at each of its keyboards and a bellows extending to several yards. Concertinas are rarely heard now at the end of the century, except occasionally with Morris dancing troupes. I heard somewhere that they are still made at a workshop in the Midlands for export to Bolivia, almost the only remaining market for them.

From concertinas he jumped to bell-ringing, to recall another musical variety act presented by an Indian lady who played handbells, temple bells and tubular bells, backed by a chorus line of girls bearing strings of bells round their necks, hips, waists and ankles, and who were conducted like an orchestra.

A year or so later it became customary for him to take me to the Penge or Croydon Empire theatres whenever a variety show was presented. We saw most of the celebrated acts of the day, including Gracie Fields, George Robey, Harry Tate and Harry Lauder, not to overlook Jack Hylton and his stage band, a show in itself, often occupying an entire bill. After the performance my grandfather would sometimes reminisce about favourites of earlier times, such as Dan Leno, Fred Karno, Vesta Tilley and Little Tich.

*

It was Grandfather Hutchings who first took me to the Crystal Palace Circus, an annual event during the Christmas season, staged in the central amphitheatre. I recall with delight Togare and his lions from Hagenbeck's Zoo at Hamburg, The Great Carmo, with his baffling animal illusion acts, and Zuleika, the lady fakir who hypnotised wildly lashing crocodiles with a pass

84

of her hands. On restoring them from quiescence at the conclusion of her act, each struggling reptile needed half a dozen attendants to remove it from the ring.

Supreme in my devotion was the equestrian bareback rider Poppy Ginnett, of the circus family of many generations of the name. For as long as we had a Christmas tree at home the fairy doll at its crest was named Poppy in her honour, as I was able to tell her many years later when I had the unexpected pleasure of meeting her, as Mrs George Sanger, in her retirement.

I never managed to get to the Bertram Mills Circus at Olympia, as I suppose my parents thought that once in a season was enough of that kind of excitement for a young child. The only other circus I was taken to was during a summer holiday at Bognor Regis, where the Royal Italian Circus was appearing on stage at the local theatre. Among its acts that remain in my mind were the Cairoli Brothers, billed as musical clowns, who played trumpets and other wind instruments, and added a classic foolery routine involving a stepladder and buckets of water.

Many years afterwards, while I was living in a remote part of Provence, a nearby village was visited for a one-night stand by a small run-down circus in which a Cairoli clown proved, on enquiry, to be a cousin of the Brothers. The horses and a pair of llamas fulfilled a double role by performing in the ring and drawing the vehicles. A performing dog act was briefly interrupted when one of its members fled at the explosion of a firework and was retrieved while barking and snarling at a wild boar foraging for edible refuse in the village street, a normal winter sight in those parts. The locals had no objection to this, as it was believed that boar urine encouraged the growth of truffles in the neighbouring woods. The connection seems credible: I have heard it claimed that truffles ceased to be found in Hampshire when cottagers no longer let their pigs out to forage in the New Forest.

*

Following soon after the Crystal Palace circus season came the national livestock shows, first for pigeons, followed by poultry and rabbits, and then canaries and other birds. My grandfather first took me to them, but when I was old enough to make the journey alone I spent countless hours at each show, dawdling along the aisles of pens unhurried by an accompanying adult, and often emboldened to ask questions of exhibitors or stewards.

Grandfather had been a keen pigeon fancier in his youth, and at the first show he took me to, he began my initiation into the standards of the exhibits. I was enthralled by the diversity of their plumage patterns and colouring, and not least by the delightful names of many of the breeds, such as Archangel, Hyacinth, Jacobin, Satinette, Florentine and Damascene. In later years he had cultivated show chrysanthemums – white as snow, and as large as dinner plates, he told me – in the conservatory of his house in the East End. My father told me that when he was a schoolboy the oil heater in the conservatory once exploded on the evening before the cherished blooms were due to be exhibited, and he and his brothers had to spend hours cleaning them petal by petal.

Grandfather was a meticulous gardener, but my father decried his orderly methods in favour of what he liked to call 'the natural setting', which involved a preponderance of evergreens. He was never known to use a spade: instead, he scratched the surface between plants with a handfork. His annual weekend of gardening in late spring was limited to weeding and cutting back, the produce of which was piled until dry enough to make a bonfire. Nothing was ever put back into the soil, and in time its level sank perceptively below that of the neighbouring gardens and grew an increasingly plentiful covering of moss.

*

I was soon infected by my grandfather's enthusiasm for steam traction engines, still a common sight on the roads during the 1920s, and indeed some of the finest restored examples seen at rallies in later times were built during that decade. He explained to me the different characteristics of the Foden and the Sentinel, the principal load-carrying vehicles of the period, and of the draught-towing machines of Aveling, Rushton and Burrel.

Woodside was on a favoured route for fairground cavalcades travelling between venues. On one lucky occasion we saw Victory, the magnificent showman's engine built by Burrel in 1920 and latterly restored and conserved in the Thursford Collection in Norfolk. During the following school holiday we saw Victory in action at the fair in South Norwood Park, generating current for the rides and the great Gavioli organ.

The Woodside Brickworks operated two traction engines at that time: a load-bearing Foden and a draught-hauling Aveling. Both of them often passed me on my way to school, and on one memorable occasion the Aveling suffered a minor explosion that scattered bits across the road. The driver shouted to me to stand clear, and after tinkering with the mechanism he eventually proceeded. By this time I was late for school, as I habitually timed myself to arrive only just before the bell, to avoid harassment. My excuse for lateness was disbelieved, and I was reported to my parents for untruthfulness.

*

Oddly, as it now seems to me, my grandfather's addiction to steam road vehicles did not extend to rail locomotives, although he served the London & North Western Railway for over 50 years. He succeeded his father in the specialised activity of tunage valuation. This involved accounting for the transit of rolling stock owned by or leased to outside concerns, such as coal merchants, and many others in an age when heavy and bulky materials were not normally transported by road. The goods wagons were assembled in marshalling yards by shunting engines, to be segregated close to their ultimate destination. The loaded journey was by main line and was charged at standard tariff, whereas the 'outward or returned empty' rates varied according to convenience and traffic conditions. This difference could give rise to controversies, and when legal confrontation ensued, my grandfather, as the Company's tunage valuer, would appear in court as its expert witness.

*

Grandfather Hutchings had no brothers or sisters, but three sons, of whom my father was the youngest, and two daughters. The eldest son and daughter both emigrated to New Zealand early in life, where they had many children and grandchildren, hence I have many more relatives there than in England. I have never met any of them, and judging from my parents' experience of visits from them and their exacting and extended demands of hospitality, I am thankful to have been spared.

The younger daughter, my Aunt Beatie, was a familiar figure during my childhood with her son, my Cousin George, who was about my age. She took us to several performances at the London Palladium, then the unchallenged summit of variety acts, and introduced me to the fairground attractions of Brighton and Southend-on-Sea. These were varied, and often surprising, in those days: added to the 'rides', coconut shies and shooting galleries would be marquees offering luridly promised wonderful sights to be viewed within by paying customers. These were often 'freak shows', human or animal, the latter sometimes living but more often preserved. Then there were the skilled sideshow performances, such as sword-swallowers, fireaters, snake-charmers and contortionists.

My father's brother, Victor, preferred an outdoor life to the clerical career for which he was parentally destined, and became a tallyman in the London Docks. In due course he was elected to union office, and eventually became a Labour Councillor for an East End ward. Our grandfather was so incensed by this act of 'treachery', as he saw it, that he never spoke to him or of him again. Ironically, Uncle Victor's son, my Cousin Albert, grew up to become a staunch Conservative.

*

On one expedition with my grandfather, we crossed the High Street and turned into Auckland Road, which ran parallel to South Norwood Hill but at a lower level. I found it somewhat disappointing: mostly woodland and orchards, and only a few large houses. There was an imposing redbrick church, where later on I would attend High Mass during my Anglo-Catholic bout of piety in early adolescence. Had I been aware of it at the time, there was an alternative venue much nearer home: the chapel of Father Tooth's Orphanage at Woodside Green. As a young priest during the early years of the Oxford Movement, he enjoyed the distinction of serving a prison sentence for breaches of the Ornaments Rubric of the Church of England.

Grandfather's objective in taking this Auckland Road route was not the Crystal Palace on this occasion, but the lower entrance to its grounds in Penge in order to see the life-size group of model dinosaurs there, of which photographs had recently been published. We were disappointed to find them closed to the public, as they had been since the war, and were destined to remain closed until after the next war. I eventually viewed them some 40 years later, long after my grandfather's decease.

*

Opposite the Palace Grounds gate was a secondhand cycle business that dealt mostly in non-standard machines of various kinds. On its forecourt were tandems and tricycles, and even single-wheel monocycles.

Riding tricycles (as distinct from delivery versions) have changed little during the varied evolution of the bicycle, and at the century's end they still resist long-threatened extinction. Each time I have seen one being ridden I have always thought 'there goes the final survivor' – until the next one appears.

The load-carrying tricycle, then widely used by tradesmen, all but disappeared from the streets soon after the Second World War. For some probably sound reason the carrying chamber was always in front, with a rod attachment in lieu of handlebars, and the saddle and the pedals at the rear. The most conspicuous of these tricycles during my childhood were those ridden by Walls ice cream salesman, who patrolled residential streets at walking pace, ringing their bells continuously. It took some time for my mother to accept the need to go outside the house to purchase from them – rarely, since ice cream was still to her and to many a special occasion luxury. Fortunately, she had faith in the Walls product, but not in that of their itinerant rivals, Eldorado, which earned her outright condemnation, but I never knew the reason why. Ice cream then was limited to vanilla and strawberry flavours, divided equally when bought in bricks, but penny cornets and twopenny wafers came only with vanilla. Later on a third variety – pistachio – was added to family-size bricks, but I was disappointed to find that, despite its distinctive green colour, it tasted much the same as vanilla.

Another hawker who announced his progress with a bell along our road was the muffin man, with his wares covered with a cloth on a tray borne on his head. In reality he sold only crumpets, and not muffins.

Tradesmen's bicycles with load-carrying racks mounted in front were commonly seen, and it seems surprising that they have virtually disappeared in modern times, except as period 'props' in films and television dramas. During the 1920s the carrying capacity was greatly increased by reducing the size of the front wheel, which at first seemed oddly reminiscent of the pennyfarthing cycle in reverse.

As we were leaving the forecourt, the proprietor was demonstrating a monocycle. When I asked why they lacked handlebars, I was told it was because their riders needed to have both hands free for their juggling performance.

*   *   *

The last outing with my grandfather before the next school term was by train to the Crystal Palace High Level station, not to visit the Palace but to call at the Beulah Spa Hotel, where he had arrangements to make for a function of the Ratepayers' Association. While he was occupied in the manager's office, I enjoyed looking at a collection of framed prints of the Spa in its nineteenth-century heyday as a fashionable health resort and pleasure ground, which once housed a menagerie. By this time the fine building, with its broad Italianate frontage, showed signs of long neglect. It was demolished after the Second World War, but the public house bearing the name survives on the site.

Patrolling on the station platform, the stationmaster greeted my grandfather deferentially, remarking on the medallion worn, when travelling by rail, on his lapel. This gave him free travel throughout the London & North Western network, a privilege extending into his retirement, and he was generally accorded a similar fare-paying exemption on other companies' lines.

The stationmaster was wearing his smartly-tailored company livery uniform, with a rose in his buttonhole. On formal occasions, my grandfather told me, as when receiving travelling royalty or civic dignitaries, the appropriate outfit would be full morning dress, with a silk 'topper'.

Sir Noël Coward is said to have been asked, as a matter of etiquette, whether red or white blooms should be worn by men. 'White carnations are worn by wedding guests and on white-tie occasions; red carnations may be worn on dinner jackets,' he was reported as replying. 'A rose is worn by stationmasters,' he added as an afterthought.

This last dictum affirmed a minor Victorian social stratification that survived unchanged into the 1920s. Stationmasters were representative of a sub-class that comprised such as butlers, head gamekeepers, and solicitors' clerks, whose intermediary function was to communicate between upper and lower elements – and the rose buttonhole consistently distinguished them.

For these minor functionaries many public houses then had 'private bars', secluded enclaves with separate entrance, served by way of a discreet hatch rather than at a bar in general public view. Private bars are now long forgotten, together with ladies' bars, and the 'bottle and jug' door for off-sales for home consumption. The saloon bar became the latterday lounge. Dominos were the favoured game in private bars, shove-ha'penny in public bars, and many saloon bars provided billiard tables. Snooker was regarded as a lowly second-best substitute for billiards. Darts, although an ancient game, had yet to re-appear in pubs.

The bowler hat was also then a distinguishing badge of the rose buttonhole wearers: it was only later, during the 1930s, that it became the conventional headwear of the City of London 'gentry', who still sported top hats to their daily duties in the early 1920s. My father, like most clerical workers then, wore felt trilbies, arbitrarily grey, with the snap brims turned down at the front and up at the rear. When I questioned him about this custom I was told that to wear the brim turned down all round would suggest an irresponsible Bohemian-style outlook on life. Some few felt-hat wearers preferred Homburgs, with upturned brims stiffened with black braid, but my father decried them as pretentious.

*   *   *

The new term at Lister House was heralded with a freshly painted signboard outside, announcing that the new proprietor and headmaster was Captain Alastair Cassidy, MC, DSO, MA (Cantab). At morning assembly on the first day, newly appointed members of the teaching staff were presented: Mr Arnold, a youthful person with a downy moustache and severe acne, and two part-time auxiliaries, Mr Robinson to teach wood-work to the older boys, and Sergeant Peacock, who would be taking drill and gymnastics on Friday afternoons in the church hall in lieu of Miss Smith. All the former staff members were retained.

Among the many innovations to emerge was a progress diary for each pupil, in which the teachers recorded observations to be countersigned by a parent every weekend. This proved the undoing of young Mr Arnold, who was prone to facetious remarks in his diary notes. He was banished from the scene at mid-term, and his subsequent career was unknown to us. I last saw him as a volunteer bus driver during the General Strike in 1926, with a policeman seated beside him.

Mr Robinson was earnestly dedicated to his craft, a City and Guilds gold medallist and a patient teacher. Only one breach of his rules would disturb his habitual equanimity: he could not tolerate sandpaper applied unless wrapped around an offcut. The sight of this infringement, and this alone, provoked him to violent reproof.

Sergeant Peacock was a gruff and hearty man who arrived for his sessions dressed in a vast leather topcoat with a fur collar, and riding a motorcycle with an unoccupied sidecar. Under the leather coat he wore gym kit, the vest bearing a crown and the initials APTS, which we were told stood for the Army Physical Training School. He was easy-going, but he could not coun-tenance nail-biting. Fingers were inspected weekly, and anyone whose nails offended was publicly upbraided and ridiculed. This would probably not be approved by a modern psychologist as the appropriate way to treat the problem, but it seemed to be effective in many cases, at least for a time.

The new headmaster proved to be a teacher of exceptional calibre, with the ability to enthuse interest in everything he taught. Indeed, I never came across his equal in this respect throughout my schooldays. His weakness was lack of continuity, and he was prone to disconcerting changes of direction and improvisation, often at such short notice as to produce chaos. His announcement of school sports to take place the following day, for example, gave parents no time to provide running kit. Another cause of confusion was the innovation of a weekly visit to the public baths to encourage swimming, but this varied between Monday, Tuesday or Thursday, without prior notice. The baths had first- and second-class pools, but the latter looked far from salubrious as we passed its doorway. An annual gala took place at the baths, with swimming races and demon-strations of acrobatic diving and lifesaving by members of the staff. A hastily organised school concert – although 'organised' is hardly the appropriate word – without prior rehearsal was little short of a disaster. As its conclusion he lined up the senior pupils on the platform and announced that they would sing the school song, 'Land of Hope and Glory'. The bemused choir stood there with voiceless open mouths, not knowing the words and, until that moment, unaware that Lister House had ever had a school song.

*

Captain Cassidy might well have adjusted his spontaneous enthusiasms to practical limits with further experience of man-agement as distinct from teaching, but more implacable prob-lems were looming. These involved the behaviour of his adopted son, who joined as a pupil from the beginning of the term. He was small and gnome-like, with wizened features, a harsh voice and hectoring manner, and was frenetically active. We never knew his first name, and none of us ventured to ask about it. The teachers referred to him as Master Cassidy, and this was how he called himself when issuing his orders and demands, always in the third person. This irritating habit, and his frequent practice of sneaking or threatening to sneak if his browbeating demands were questioned, were sorely resented. The only benefit from his presence was a dramatic reduction of bullying and taunting, which he regarded as solely his prerogative. For me, his most loathsome trait was the collar button of his shirts, always visible above an untidily knotted necktie. The offending buttons were linen covered, with four brass-rimmed holes for the stitches. From as far back as I could recall I suffered a phobic horror of such buttons. The only shop I dreaded being taken into was a bakery where my mother would sometimes buy iced buns topped with glacé cherries, known as 'fancies'. The two assistants there wore overalls secured at the front with these buttons, and knowing that the hands that had touched them would serve our purchase was a desperately nauseating crisis. The harrowing ordeal eventually terminated when my Aunt May remarked on dirty fingernails behind the counter, and from then on our 'fancies' were shopped elsewhere.

One boy alone could stand up to his blustering: this was Jack Thwaites, a new pupil with a ventriloquial talent for voice imitation. His parents ran the men's outfitters shop in the High Street.

Several other newcomers this term were shopkeepers' children: there were Ivor and Christine Griffith, whose parents were pork butchers, Annie Feldwick, the undertaker's daughter, and Grace Todd, from one of the fish and chip shops. She was always neatly and cleanly turned-out, despite which she still bore the smell of her parents' trade. Another new pupil was Marie Latour, a French girl who lived in one of the few houses in Portland Road, with a monkey puzzle tree in its front garden. She brought a sense of glamour to the scene with her adult hairstyle, flared pleated skirts and smart patent leather shoes.

Despite his bluster, I think that Master Cassidy was apprehensive of losing a confrontation with the boys, and he vented much of his spleen on the girls. His persecution of them grew increasingly extreme, and he began to single out individuals during the mid-morning break and chase them into the back garden, which was strictly out of bounds to the rest of us. His quarries managed to elude him or hide, until one morning one of them came back to class in tears. Then, a few days later, another. His next victim was the little French girl, Marie. She came back screaming, and his face bore fresh scratch marks. He was dismissed to Captain Cassidy's study, and she was taken home by Young Miss Smith.

The miscreant was absent from assembly the next morning, and never reappeared at school. His disappearance, and the events preceding it, were never referred to there or at home. I might never have learnt anything further about the encounter had not adult curiosity, many years after, prompted me to refer to the newspaper files at the public library reference department. I learnt that when he was brought before the juvenile court he was remanded in police custody to appear at the county court, as documentary evidence presented revealed his age to be 18, not half that, as had been claimed by his adoptive parents. A specialist medical witness explained that the accused suffered from a retarded growth and mental development condition that had not, however, inhibited the onset of puberty. The changes entered against him were indecent assault and attempted rape. The subsequent few issues of the newspaper were missing from the file, and so I failed to unravel the case to its outcome.

*

Captain Cassidy's downfall and departure occurred so rapidly after his adopted son's disgrace that there must have been a link between the two events. I can only speculate that the deception revealed in court led to questions about the *bona fides* of his other claims. My first awareness that an unusual train of events was afoot was at breakfast one morning, when two loud knocks at the front door announced the postal delivery. In those days one knock heralded regular mail, two knocks if a signature was required. Readers who are unaware of this long-discontinued practice may also be surprised to learn that at that time postmen wore peaked caps and smart uniforms with red piped tunics and trousers pressed to sharp creases down the sides, instead of at the front.

My father's registered letter brought a grave look to his face and a whispered exchange with my mother in the next room. I retrieved the discarded envelope later: it was postmarked from Cambridge. He left saying that he was going down the road to speak to our neighbour Mr Tottem. When they called back together he said that they were bound for Lister House, and that he would phone his office that he would not be going in that day.

When I returned home at teatime, my father told me that tomorrow would be a school holiday. When passing Lister House next day on a walk with Speedy Winter, we saw a paper attached to the board outside announcing that the school was closed until further notice. My parents told me nothing, and exchanged cautionary glances when I asked. That I was able to piece together subsequent events was due to older boys who succeeded in overhearing their parents discussing them.

It transpired that the initial step arose from a chance meeting between my father and Mr Arnold, the young teacher who had left Lister House under a cloud. He had commented that Captain Cassidy seemed oddly ignorant of the geography and colleges of Cambridge, of which he claimed to be a graduate. This had prompted my father to send an enquiry to the university authorities, which brought the reply that no Alastair Cassidy had ever graduated there.

Meanwhile, Mr Tottem had been independently engaged in

research, prompted by the MC, DSO claim, which he said were shown in the wrong order. War Office records revealed that the Cassidy wartime Army service was as a non-combatant school-teacher: he was never commissioned, had been awarded no decorations, and secured his teaching appointment due to previous employment at a mission school. Further investigation identified him as a lapsed Anglican priest.

When long afterwards I was at last able to broach the subject with my father, he brushed aside the false claims of rank and decorations. What upset him, and still rankled, was the scandalous impiety of wearing an unearned degree hood in church. The only mitigating aspect was that the vicar, my father's old antagonist, had been taken in by the deception.

*   *   *

So concluded an epoch, not only for the school but also for me, as it soon transpired. A 'For Sale' board appeared outside Lister House, and the Cassidys departed stealthily, leaving its contents and a mountain of debts behind them. They were eventually rumoured to be running a boarding house in Brighton.

My education was not interrupted. During the vacation I had gained a place at the old grammar school in Croydon, soon to be calling itself a public day school, with new buildings and a new headmaster, as well as a crop of newly created 'ancient traditions'.

During the same gap we moved house 'across the railway lines' to the pretentious suburb of Addiscombe. This I disliked from the first, and the changes that came with it. Our sitting room became the lounge, dinner moved from midday to evening, the *Daily Mail* was superseded by the *Daily Telegraph*, and my parents gave up whist and took to bridge. The transformation into the middle-class ethos was instantaneous and without any discussion – it just came with the new address.

My only compensation was that I gained something precious I lacked at Woodside: from my new bedroom window, looking between the Lombardy poplars that skirted the railway line, I could enjoy the vista of the Crystal Palace.

*   *   *

Even years later I witnessed the great fire that destroyed the Crystal Palace in 1936. I sensed that the agonising spectacle marked the definitive end of my childhood and adolescent years, and I also felt overshadowed by a foreboding of other disasters impending. The war-to-come was already being rehearsed in Spain, a localised conflict that effected a deep emotional involvement in many of my generation. I recall a Chelsea party that Christmas, at which a brash young barrister defended Franco's 'fight to establish the rule of law'. Somebody countered angrily, 'So he starts it with an armed rebellion against a democratically elected government!' I cannot remember, after so long, who said it, but it might well have been me.

* * * * *

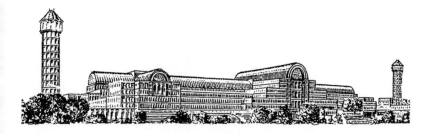